REGIMENTAL BADGES

By the same author

THE PERFORATED MAN

MILITARY CUSTOMS

REGIMENTAL MASCOTS AND PETS

Regimental Badges

First Edition

MAJOR T. J. EDWARDS, M.B.E., F.R.HIST.S.
Member of the Society for Army Historical Research

Reprint

ERNEST BENN LIMITED
LONDON & TONBRIDGE · 1980

First Edition published by Gale & Polden, 1951
Reprinted by Charles Knight 1972

This reprint published in 1980 by
Ernest Benn Limited
25 New Street Square, London, EC4A 3JA
& Sovereign Way, Tonbridge, Kent, TN9 1RW

© *Charles Knight & Company Limited 1972*

Printed in Great Britain by
Brown Knight & Truscott Ltd,
Tonbridge, Kent.

CONTENTS

YEOMANRY

vi

vii

TERRITORIAL ARMY UNITS WITH DIFFERENT BADGES

ADMINISTRATIVE DEPARTMENT AND CORPS

x

FOREWORD

THIS BOOK deals only with cap badges. It was compiled during the years 1946-1950, a transitional period when a number of regiments and corps were modifying their badges and some were modifying or changing their regimental or unit titles, especially those of the Territorial Army, on conversion from one arm to another. Although efforts were made to keep abreast of these changes, it is realized that this has not been done in all cases, particularly in those which were in the process of alteration at the time of publication.

In these circumstances I would be grateful if errors of any description could be brought to my notice, to enable them to be corrected in a later edition.

I take this opportunity of recording my thanks and appreciation of the work done by Mr. Arthur L. Kipling, of Gale & Polden Ltd., a member of the Society for Army Historical Research, in connection with the information dealing with Yeomanry badges, which he has compiled as a result of his research into the subject. This has been a most difficult task, and Mr. Kipling is to be congratulated on the excellent result of his labours.

A book of this nature could not have been compiled without the kindly assistance of numerous Commanding Officers and other officers of Regiments and Corps, who have readily supplied me with all details that were requested. This also applies to Commandants of Schools and others whose help I sought either in obtaining badges or verifying abstruse points connected with them. To all these I gratefully acknowledge much assistance, and also Major L. M. Arnold, the War Office (Ordnance 17) who very kindly placed at my disposal the sealed patterns of badges for checking.

I wish to mention particularly the help given me by Mr. L. R. Brandham, manager of the London Branch of Messrs. J. R. Gaunt & Son Ltd., 5 Warwick Street, Regent Street, London, W.1. He has an extensive knowledge of badges, acquired through long years of devoted service to this well-known firm of badge-makers. Besides lending many badges for drawing he has brought to notice several points that could only be known to one with a most intimate knowledge of the subject.

My thanks are also due to Messrs. Joseph Starkey Ltd., 16 Beak Street, Regent Street, W.1, and Messrs. Firmin & Sons Ltd., 8 Cork Street, W.1, and Messrs. Hawkes & Co., 1 Savile Row, W.1, for the loan of badges.

Mr. A. S. White, M.M., F.R.Hist.S., War Office Librarian, kindly "vetted" the proof, and I have benefited from his extensive knowledge of all things military, which he placed at my disposal in the compilation of this work.

T. J. E.

"SOMLI,"
THAMES DITTON, SURREY
August, 1950

DESCRIPTION

In describing the badges popular language has been used, except in a few instances where heraldic terms appeared to be the better medium.

LORD CLIFFORD: Might I know thee by thy Household Badge ?

EARL OF WARWICK: Now, by my father's badge, old Nevill's crest, the rampant bear chained to the ragged staff, this day I'll wear aloft in my burgonet.

(2 King Henry VI, Act V, Scene 1)

REGIMENTAL BADGES, like regimental titles, very often epitomize a considerable amount of history. As shown in the above quotation from Shakespeare, the original purpose of badges was to assist identification; the granting of badges in commemoration of great deeds is a development from the original idea. But badges are centuries older than Shakespeare, and to commence at the beginning we must go back to the dawn of history.

The evolution of regimental badges is wrapped up, to a certain extent, with the various devices employed to achieve distinction between opposing armies, such as the wearing of twigs of trees, pieces of paper, or a handful of grass in the hat as distinguishing badges, in view of which it will be necessary to trace the use of these simple devices until national uniform became so different that that alone was normally sufficient to show who was friend and who was foe.

Primitive Times

In the days of early man, clothing, if any, proved insufficient as an effective means of identifying the various families, tribes and races. Some rapid means of identification was essential in combat on any scale. Mistakes due to similarity of uniform have been made in engagements of quite modern times. To overcome his difficulty primitive man painted on his body the image of some animal or bird with which he was familiar and whose qualities he considered he possessed or wished to acquire. For instance, the fleet of foot painted the figure of a galloping horse or a bird in flight, the strong painted a lion or a bear, and the wise an owl or a serpent. In this practice we also see the origin of heraldry, which is much concerned with badges.

"Heraldry, in its essence," states G. W. Eve in "Heraldry as Art," "began when man first used natural forms to symbolize and ascribe to himself those qualities—strength, courage, cunning —which he had full cause to recognize in the beasts with whom he struggled for existence; when he produced, as well as he could, their ferocious aspect, to strike terror into his human enemies, while satisfying his own warlike vanity, and so adopted them as badges or even as totems."

This family badge or sign was also reproduced on the tent or other form of dwelling-place, and when they went to battle it was roughly carved in wood and fixed to a pole, so that when held aloft the family fighting beneath it could be identified. Herein is the origin of regimental Standards, Guidons and Colours, whose original purpose was identification.

It is not difficult to appreciate that in those early days, when superstition played a large part in the life of the people, that the badge or totem of a persistently successful family or tribe would acquire an atmosphere of veneration and give rise to a belief in its power to lead to victory. Such an attitude the Roman soldier adopted towards his eagle Standards.

What are considered to be the "Regimental Badges" of the Children of Israel are those mentioned in the 49th chapter of Genesis : "Judah is a lion's whelp . . . Issachar is a strong ass . . . Dan shall be a serpent . . . Joseph is a fruitful bough . . . Benjamin shall ravin as a wolf." In the Chinese Book of War, written about 500 B.C., we find that they had banners on which were figures of dragons, white tigers, red sparrows, snakes and tortoises. The ancient Athenians bore on their ensigns the figure of an owl, the bird sacred to Minerva, the protectress of the city. The

Thebans used a sphinx in memory of the monster overcome by Œdipus. The Romans adopted the eagle as their badge and put it on their ensigns, in allusion to the idea that as the eagle was lord of the air so they were lords of the earth. It is believed that Napoleon introduced the eagle Standards into the French army for the same reason.

In ancient times the headdress of opposing armies was usually different, but as in battle it was often removed, either forcibly by the enemy or otherwise, some other means of distinction had to be devised. In ancient Greece the "Word" or password was first used, selected by the commander. He would choose the name of some deity worshipped by his followers, or some good omen which he communicated to his officers, who passed it on to the soldiers. This, however, sometimes led to fatal consequences in battle because the men, by much questioning among themselves, often became confused and not only killed each other but disclosed the "Word" to the enemy. To remedy this a visible distinction was introduced, such as nodding the head, waving arms or clashing weapons in a particular manner. The ancient Romans seem to have relied mainly on their general difference in dress, but a "Word" was always given.

A very early instance in our own land of a badge being employed to distinguish an army and which is now used as a regimental badge is the leek, which Cadwallader ordered his men to wear so that they could recognize each other when he gained a great victory over the Saxons in 640. The leek is, of course, the regimental badge of the Welsh Guards.

Norman Conquest and Middle Ages

The famous Bayeux tapestry depicts in a series of about eighty scenes the Norman account of the battle of Hastings and the events leading up to it. It is regarded as a contemporary account, having been executed between 1066 and the end of the eleventh century. A study of the knights' banners reveals that a number of devices were employed to secure the identification of individuals. The banners differ in the number of their tails and they contain balls, crosses and other details in varied arrangements to secure the same end.

With the introduction of body armour, man began to cover himself and his horse as much as possible to exclude the likelihood of suffering hurt from any source. About the twelfth century this "covering up" had reached the point where nothing of the man and very little of his horse could be seen. This, of course, put him into the same position as primitive naked man, in that in the din and dust of battle the difficulty of distinguishing friend from foe was almost insuperable. The need for some method of rapid identification became, therefore, a matter of life and death.

"From the circumstance that it first found its special use in direct connection with military equipments, knightly exercises and the mêlée of actual battle, medieval heraldry has also been styled Armoury. Men wore the ensigns of heraldry about their persons, embroidered upon the garments that partially covered their armour, and so they called them Coats-of-Arms; they bore these same ensigns on their shields and they called them Shields-of-Arms; and in their armorial banners and pennons they again displayed the very same insignia, floating in the wind high above their heads, from the shafts of their lances" (Charles Boutell in "English Heraldry").

It is clear that medieval nobility, having found themselves similarly situated as early man, adopted his methods for securing identification, with this difference—that instead of ornamenting their naked bodies with painted figures they decorated their outer clothing and shields with badges.

In view of the fact that the use of personal badges was fairly universal in Europe about this time, it was quite possible that in opposing armies would be found knights wearing very similar

4

badges, so that their general appearance was practically identical. Such a situation called for further measures to secure national identification at a glance, which was no doubt responsible for Richard II issuing the following Article of War in 1385:

"Every man of what estate, condition or nation he may be, so that he be of our party, shall wear a large sign of the Arms of St. George before and another behind, upon peril that if he be hurt or slain in default thereof, he who shall hurt or slay him shall no penalty pay for it; and that no enemy shall bear the said sign of St. George whether he be a prisoner or otherwise, upon pain of death."

Richard was a young man at this time and the counties about London had recently been disturbed by Wat Tyler's rebellion. More serious than this, however, was the scheming of the young King's uncle, Thomas, Duke of Gloucester, who formed a party of the more important nobles to oppose him. This led to civil war. It was, therefore, a matter of some importance to the King to know at a glance who was on his side, which this very plain red Cross of St. George must have proclaimed.

The battle of Agincourt was fought on 25th October, 1415, St. Crispin's Day, and the following conversation between King Henry V and Fluellen, as given in Shakespeare (*King Henry V*, Act IV, Scene 7) shows that the Welshmen wore their leek badges at that famous victory, as well as on a previous occasion:

"FLUELLEN: Your grandfather of famous memory, an 't please your Majesty, and your great uncle Edward the Plack Prince of Wales, as I have read in the chronicles, fought a most prave pattle here in France.

"KING HENRY: They did, Fluellen.

"FLUELLEN: Your Majesty says very true. If your Majesties is remembered of it, the Welshmen did goot service in a garden where leeks did grow, wearing leeks in their Monmouth caps; which, your Majesty knows, to this hour is an honourable padge

B   5

of the service; and, I do believe, your Majesty takes no scorn to wear the leek upon St. Tavy's Day.

"KING HENRY: I wear it for a memorable honour; for I am Welsh, you know, good countryman."

The Wars of the Roses (1450-85) take their name from two rose badges: the White Rose of York and the Red Rose of Lancaster, both of which are worn today by some of our regiments. Besides the rose uniform badges we are also familiar with the roses worn on "Minden Day" by the "Minden" regiments in memory of the tradition that the British infantry regiments, on passing across Minden Heath to meet the French, plucked roses from the briars and stuck them in their coats and hats on that 1st August, 1759. The Royal Northumberland Fusiliers wear red and white roses in their hats and on their drums and Colours on St. George's Day. In 1881 all English infantry regiments that had not a special badge on their Colours were ordered to assume the Union Rose. This badge has gradually been discontinued as a result of these regiments being granted special badges.

Tudor Period

In 1512 Henry VIII, in his orders to the Earl of Shrewsbury, directed: "And ye then to delyver for us in our name, to every of our subjects so retayned in your company, suche badges, tokyns or lyveres to were [wear], as by you shall be thought most convenient for the Same, which we will they shall were for the same purpose."* In 1544 "Bluff King Hal" issued another order which must have given his troops a comic-opera appearance, while achieving the much-desired distinction. It runs: "Every man to provide a payer of hose for every one of his men, the right hose to be red and the left to be blew, with one stripe

---

* Grose, "Military Antiquities," I, p. 324.

of three fingers brode of red upon the outside leg from the stocke downwards."* This seems to be an early attempt at uniformity in dress, the absence of which led also to the wearing of coloured scarves, flowers, twigs of oak, etc., about the ordinary civilian clothes.

In 1540 Henry VIII had a very troubled time; a war with Scotland broke out in 1540 and lasted until the battle of Solway Moss in November, 1542, when Henry defeated the Scots so decisively that it ended the war. James V of Scotland, however, had allied himself to France, so that Henry now had to contend with a foe in the south. In 1544, however, Henry sent a large English army to Scotland to subdue the Lowlands. This done, he prepared an expedition against France. For this expedition "Statutes and Ordynances for the Warre" were framed. These are reproduced in the *Journal of the Society for Army Historical Research* (VII, p. 222), the forty-eighth article reading as follows and showing the persistence of the St. George's Cross as the National Badge:

> "For theym that beare not a bond
> or a crosse of sayncte George."

"Also that every man goyng in hostyng or battayle, of what estate condition or nation he be, of the kynges partie and hoste, excepte he be a bysshop or officer of armys, beare a Crosse of saynt George, sufficient and large, vppon the peine that if he be wounded or slaine in the defaulte thereof, he that so woundeth or sleeth him, shall beare no payne therefore. And if he for any cause passe the bondes of the fielde, that then he beare openly a crosse of saynt George, vpon peyne to be imprisoned and punyshed at the Kinges pleasure. And that no souldier bear no cognisance but the Kinges and his captaines, vpon paine of death. And that no enemy beare the sayde signe of Saint George, but

---

* Grose, "Military Antiquities," I, p. 325. This uniform appeared in the Field of Cloth of Gold scenes at Aldershot Tattoo, 1938.

7

if he be prisoner and in warde of his maister, vpon payne of deathe."

An instance of badges being worn on uniform during the reign of Queen Elizabeth is recorded in *The Fugger News Letters* relating to an expedition to Zeeland under Norris. Under date "Cologne, September 6, 1585," after describing the arrival of the troops at Flushing, a letter adds: "Among the English are thirty-five Captains, each with a hundred and twenty men in his company. They are all smart men in red coats, bearing the badge of the Queen of England." Unfortunately, the particular badge is not described, as the Queen had several badges.

The idea of Company Badges, which persists today in the Foot Guards alone, seems to have come into vogue about the beginning of the seventeenth century, for we find in "Animadversions of War," by Ward, published in 1639, in the chapter dealing with the "Office and Duty of a Colonel of a Regiment," that "hee ought to have all the Colours of his Regiment to be alike both in colour and in fashion to avòide confusion so that the soldiers may discerne their owne Regiment from the other troops, likewise, every particular Captain of his Regiment may have some small distinctions in their Colours, as their Armes, or some embleme, or the like so that one Company may be discerned from another." Herein we see a definite use of private badges (Armes) for regimental and company distinction, from which regimental badges evolved.

Commonwealth

Regarding the wearing of scarves as distinguishing badges, Sir Charles Firth, in his "Cromwell's Army," relates that at the battle of Edgehill (23rd October, 1642) during the Civil War, Sir Faithful Fortescue's Troop in the Parliament forces deserted in a body to the King's army, but about seventeen or eighteen of them were killed by their new allies owing to their negligence in not throwing away their orange-coloured scarves, which were the badge of the Parliament Army. At the battle of Marston Moor

8

(2nd July, 1644) Lord Fairfax of the Parliamentary force was surrounded by the Royalist cavalry, but escaped from them by the simple expedient of removing the piece of white paper from his hat, which was the badge of the Parliamentarians on that occasion. When the New Model of the Commonwealth came into being in 1645 the whole of the army was clothed in scarlet coats, regiments being distinguished by the colour of their facings, which corresponded to their title—*e.g.*, the Red Regiment wore red facings, the Blue Regiment wore blue facings, etc. etc. We find something of an echo of this system in the present-day titles of a few regiments, such as The Blues, The Bays, The Greys, The Buffs, The Green Howards and The Black Watch.

When Charles II established the Standing Army in 1661 he granted to each company of his Foot Guards one of his Royal Badges to be borne upon their Colour. These badges are still borne in rotation on the Regimental Colours of each battalion, the change taking place at each new issue of Colours. Colonels of other regiments followed the royal example and placed their own personal badges on the Colours of their regiments.

When the Household Cavalry was established in 1661, the drummers and trumpeters wore badges of the Royal Cypher embroidered on the breast and back of their coats.

Field Marks and Words

Roger Boyle, 1st Earl of Orrery, was a soldier of much experience during the period of the Civil War, Commonwealth, and the early years of the Restoration. Not long before he died he wrote "A Treatise of the Art of War" (1677), wherein he gives some space to the use of distinguishing badges between armies. In the chapter on "Battels" he says:

"Before the fighting of a Battel, the Field Mark, and the Field Word, ought still to be given to every one of your men; the first is, That you may be able to distinguish afar off, who are

9

Friends and who are Enemies. . . . In the hurry and confusion of a fight, private soldiers must have some very apparent Field Mark to enable them to distinguish Foes from Friends, else much mischief may too easily ensue.

"And because such Field Marks, wherever you place them, are not still visible on all sides of the head or body of every one who wears them, the Field Word is also given; For it often happens that in a Battel, the Field Mark is by accident lost by many out of their helmets or hats, and then if they had not the Field Word, they might be killed by those of their own party who knew them not personally.

"Besides, the Field Mark, of each army is seen by all of both armies before they engage, and the matter of it, being to be had in all places by private soldiers (as a green branch, a piece of Fern, or a handful of Grass, or a piece of white paper, etc.). If you rout your enemy, he may, while he is pursued, take off his own Field Mark, put up yours instead of it, and so escape, if not do you hurt; but the Field Word he cannot know, unless it be told him by some of your own men; and therefore the giving of both before the Battel must never be omitted.

"I remember once when some forces I had the honour to command, obtained, by the Blessing of God, the victory against the enemy; an officer of mine, having killed an officer of the enemy, and finding he had a good beaver, he tyed his owne helmet to his saddle bow, and put on so hastily the dead man's beaver, as he forgot to take out of it the green branch which was their Field Mark, and to put on it a White Paper which was our Field Mark, and following the execution with his sword all bloody, a Captain of Horse of my own regiment, taking him by his Field Mark for one of the enemy, and judging he had done no little slaughter by his sword being all gored to the hilt, undertook him in the pursuit, and turning about on him, before he could see his face, ran him through and through with his tuck, whereof he dyed in a few minutes."

Another well-known writer on military matters in Charles II's time was Sir James Turner, who published his "Pallas Armata" in 1683. He shows how these distinguishing badges were not confined to hats (cap-badges), but were also worn on the coats. He writes, in regard to preparing for battle: "All these things being done, the Word and the Sign should be given, and these are quickly carried through the army by the Major-Generals and the Adjutants. At such a time the Word is ordinarily a sentence (for Souldiers are no Grammarians) as, God with us, For God and the King, Our Trust is in God, and Vivat such a Prince, and the like. The Sign may be a handkerchief on the hat, or a piece of Linnen on the right or left arm, a twig of birch, an Elme, an Oak, or a Sycamore, or it may be a Fur, of what else the Prince or his General pleaseth."

Boughs or twigs in the hat seem to have been a favourite badge among English troops, and an incident during the War of the Spanish Succession, which occurred in Spain in 1707, lends colour to this view. Captain George Carleton, in his "Wars against France," records that "About eight leagues from Cuenca, at a pretty town called Huette, a party from the Duke of Berwick's, with boughs in their hats, the better to appear what they were not (for the bough in the hat is the Badge of the English, as the White Paper is the Badge of the French)."

The British carried the idea to India, where, at the battle of Wandewash (22nd January, 1760), Coote ordered: "The whole army as well European as black, are to have a green branch of the Tamarind tree, fixed in their hats and turbans; likewise upon the tops of the Colours, in order to distinguish them from the enemy."

Badges on Standards, Guidons and Colours

Perhaps what is the earliest Army List to be printed after the Restoration is Nathan Brooks's "General and Compleat List Military . . . As Establish't at the time of the review upon Putney

Heath, the First of October, 1684." From this list we obtain the description of badges borne upon the Standards, Guidons and Colours of the regiments as they were a few months before the death of Charles II. He died in February, 1685, and was succeeded by his brother James, Duke of York, as James II. The new king's coronation took place on St. George's Day, 23rd April, 1685, of which Sandford, the Herald, wrote a detailed account. From this we gather that the three Troops of Life Guards were distinguished by the colour of the "large knots of riband in their hats and on the heads of their horses; blew for the King's or First Troop, green for the Second Troop and yellow for the Third Troop." During James's reign the use of private armorial bearings by Colonels of Regiments grew apace, but it seems that they did no more than put them on the Standards, Guidons or Colours of their regiments. In the Royal Library at Windsor Castle there is a set of paintings of Standards, etc., of this period, clearly showing the Colonels' badges borne upon them. And so this practice continued until George II put a stop to it by Royal Warrant dated 1st July, 1751.*

A very fine relic of the period under consideration is the standard of Ligonier's Horse, carried at the battle of Dettingen in 1743, which now hangs in the Museum of the Royal United Service Institution. Although it must be about two hundred years old, one can still see General Sir John (later Field-Marshal Lord) Ligonier's crest upon it (a demi-lion issuing from a coronet). For many years the 7th Dragoon Guards, formerly Ligonier's, wore his crest as a uniform badge.

THE 1751 ROYAL WARRANT

Colonels of Cavalry and Infantry of the Line continued to place their personal arms on Standards, etc., until this was prohibited by Royal Warrant of 1st July, 1751. This was the first

---

* A Royal Warrant is said to have been published in 1743 giving the substance of the 1751 Warrant but has never been traced. In the Royal Library at Windsor Castle there is a copy of Regulations dated 1747, which appear to be the basis of the 1751 Warrant.

warrant of its kind to make an attempt at systematizing the uniform, Colours, headdresses and similar items.

The first paragraph reads: "No Colonel to put his Arms, Crest, Device or Livery on any part of the Appointments of the Regiment under his command."

For purposes of regimental distinction the warrant laid down certain regulations, the main of which are given here.

Infantry

This is the first Royal Warrant to mention badges for wear on headdresses. Dealing with "Grenadier Caps" it is stated that: "The front of the Grenadier Caps to be of the same colour as the facings of the regiment, with the King's Cypher embroidered and Crown over it; the little flaps to be red with the White Horse motto over it, 'Nec aspera terrent'; the back part of the Caps to be red, the turn-up to be the colour of the Front with the Number of the Regiment in the middle part behind. The Royal Regiments and the Six Old Corps differ from the foregoing Rule."

Some regiments were authorized to have badges on their Colours, Grenadier caps, drums and Bells of Arms, as shown.

The "Number of the Regiment" referred to the position held by the regiment in the official Order of Precedence. The question of the relative precedence of regiments was settled periodically, usually by Boards of General Officers.

As regards the colour of the facings, these had probably been worn by regiments long before the issue of this Royal Warrant which merely confirmed them. As regimental distinctions the system could not have been completely successful because several regiments had the same colour, or a different shade of the same colour, for facings. As this may be regarded as a milestone in the evolution of regimental badges, an extract from the warrant is appended.

13

EXTRACT FROM "GENERAL VIEW OF THE FACINGS OF THE SEVERAL MARCHING REGIMENTS OF FOOT."

Colour of the Facings	Rank and title of Ye Regiment	Distinctions In the same colour
Blue	1st or Ye Royal Regiment 4th or The King's Own Regiment 7th or Ye Royal Fusiliers 8th or The King's Regiment 18th or The Royal Irish 21st or Ye Royal North British Fusiliers 23rd or The Royal Welch Fusiliers 41st or the Invalids	
Green	2nd or The Queen's Royal Regiment 5th Regiment 11th Regiment 19th Regiment 24th Regiment 36th Regiment 39th Regiment 45th Regiment 49th Regiment	Sea green Gosling green Full green Yellowish green Willow green Deep green Full green
Buff	3rd Regiment or The Buffs 14th Regiment 22nd Regiment 27th or The Inniskilling Regiment 31st Regiment 40th Regiment 42nd Regiment 48th Regiment	 Pale buff
White	17th Regiment 32nd Regiment 43rd Regiment 47th Regiment	Greyish white
Red	33rd Regiment	
Orange	35th Regiment 6th Regiment 9th Regiment 10th Regiment	 Deep yellow Bright yellow

14

Colour of the Facings	Rank and title of Ye Regiment	Distinctions In the same colour
Orange	12th Regiment	
	13th Regiment	Philemot yellow
	15th Regiment	
	16th Regiment	
	20th Regiment	Pale yellow
Yellow	25th Regiment	Deep yellow
	26th Regiment	Pale yellow
	28th Regiment	Bright yellow
	29th Regiment	
	30th Regiment	Pale yellow
	34th Regiment	Bright yellow
	37th Regiment	
	38th Regiment	
	44th Regiment	
	46th Regiment	
Red with blue coats	Royal Regiment of Artillery	

ABSTRACT

Blue	...	...	...	...	8 regiments
Green	...	...	...	...	9 ,,
Buff	...	...	...	...	8 ,,
Yellow		...	...	...	18 ,,
White	...	...	...	...	4 ,,
Red	...	...	...	...	1 regiment
Orange		...	...	...	1 ,,
Blue with Red		...	...	...	1 ,,
					50 regiments

In addition to all regiments being ordered to wear the "Number of the Regiment" at the back of their Grenadier caps, the "Royal Regiments and six old Corps" were authorized to wear "Devices and Badges" on their Colours and elsewhere as shown in the attached table. It will be noted that some of the badges authorized for wear on the Colours have since been adopted as clothing badges and are still in use, indicating that the latter evolved from the former, thus linking them with primitive emblems.

BADGES

REGIMENT	In centre of Colours	In three corners of Second Colour	On Grenadier Caps	On Drums and Bells of Arms
1st, or The Royal Regiment.	King's Cypher within Circle of St. Andrew and Crown over it.	Thistle and Crown.	Same as centre of Colours, also White Horse with King's motto "Nec Aspera terrent" over it.	Same as centre of Colours with Number of Rank of Regiment under it.
2nd, or The Queen's Royal Regiment.	Queen's Cypher on a red ground within the Garter and Crown over it.	The Lamb.	Same as centre of Colours, also White Horse with King's motto "Nec Aspera terrent" over it.	Same as centre of Colours with Number of Rank of Regiment under it.
3rd, or The Buffs.	The Dragon.	Rose and Crown.	Same as centre of Colours, also White Horse with King's motto "Nec Aspera terrent" over it.	Same as centre of Colours with Number of Rank of Regiment under it.
4th, or The King's Own Royal Regiment.	King's Cypher on a red ground within the Garter and Crown over it.	Lyon of England.	Same as centre of Colours, also White Horse with King's motto "Nec Aspera terrent" over it.	Same as centre of Colours with Number of Rank of Regiment under it.

16

5th Regiment.	St. George killing the Dragon.	Rose and Crown.	Same as centre of Colours, also White Horse with King's motto "Nec Aspera terrent" over it.	Same as centre of Colours with Number of Rank of Regiment under it.
6th Regiment.	The Antelope.	Rose and Crown.	Same as centre of Colours, also White Horse with King's motto "Nec Aspera terrent" over it.	Same as centre of Colours with Number of Rank of Regiment under it.
7th, or the Royal Fusileers.	The Rose within the Garter and Crown over it.	The White Horse.	Same as centre of Colours, also White Horse with King's motto "Nec Aspera terrent" over it.	Same as centre of Colours with Number of Rank of Regiment under it.
8th, or The King's Regiment.	The White Horse on a red ground within the Garter and Crown over it.	King's Cypher and Crown.	Same as centre of Colours, also White Horse with King's motto "Nec Aspera terrent" over it.	Same as centre of Colours with Number of Rank of Regiment under it.
18th, or The Royal Irish.	The Harp in a blue field with Crown over it.	The Lyon of Nassau, King William the Third's Arms.	Same as centre of Colours, also White Horse with King's motto "Nec Aspera terrent" over it.	Same as centre of Colours with Number of Rank of Regiment under it.
21st, or The Royal North British Fuziliers.	The Thistle within the Circle of St. Andrew and Crown over it.	The King's Cypher and Crown.	Same as centre of Colours, also White Horse with King's motto "Nec Aspera terrent" over it.	Same as centre of Colours with Number of Rank of Regiment under it.

17

BADGES

REGIMENT	In centre of Colours	In three corners of Second Colour	On Grenadier Caps	On Drums and Bells of Arms
23rd, or The Royal Welch Fuziliers	The device of the Prince of Wales, viz., three Feathers issuing out of the Prince's Coronet.	The badges of the Black Prince, viz., Rising Sun, Red Dragon and the three Feathers in the Coronet with motto "Ich Dien."	The Feathers as in the Colours, with White Horse and motto "Nec Aspera terrent."	The three Feathers and motto "Ich Dien" with Rank of Regiment under it.
27th, or The Inniskilling Regiment.	A Castle with three turrets, St. George's Colours flying in a blue field and the name "Inniskilling" over it.	—	Same as centre of Colours with White Horse and motto.	Same as centre of Colours with Rank of Regiment under it.
41st, or The Invalids.	The Rose and Thistle on a red ground within the Garter, and Crown over it.	The King's Cypher and Crown.	Same as centre of Colours.	Same as centre of Colours.
Highland Regiment.	—	—	To wear bear-skin fur caps with the King's Cypher and Crown over it, on a red ground, in the turn-up of the flap.	—

The distinctions in the Cavalry consisted of:

Coats of Dragoon Guards to be lapelled to the waist.

Coats of Horse to be lapelled to the bottom.

Coats of Dragoons to be without lapels.

The Housings and Holster Caps to be the colour of the facings (except that those of the King's Dragoon Guards are to be red and those of 4th Horse to be buff).

The "Rank of the Regiment" or "particular badge of the Regiment" to be embroidered on the Housings.

As regards the "Rank of the Regiment" or "particular badge" being embroidered on the Housings, the "General View" lists the following:

Ranks and Titles of the several Corps of Dragoon Guards, Horse and Dragoons	*Badge or Device on the Housings and Holster Caps*	*Present Title of the Regiment*
Blue Facings		
1st or King's Regiment of Dragoon Guards	King's Cypher within the Garter and crown	1st King's Dragoon Guards
1st Horse	I.H.	4th Dragoon Guards, now forms part of 4th/7th Royal Dragoon Guards
1st or Royal Dragoons	Crest of England within the Garter	1st The Royal Dragoons
2nd or Royal North-British Dragoons	Thistle within the Circle of St. Andrew	The Royal Scots Greys
3rd or The King's Own Regiment of Dragoons	White Horse within the Garter	3rd The King's Own Hussars
5th or Royal Irish Dragoons	Harp and crown	5th Lancers now forms part of 16th/5th Lancers
Yellow Facings		
3rd Regiment of Horse or the Carabineers	III.H.	The Carabiniers now forms part of 3rd Carabiniers

Ranks and Titles of the several Corps of Dragoon Guards, Horse and Dragoons	Badge or Device on the Housings and Holster Caps	Present Title of the Regiment
6th or the Inniskilling Dragoons	Castle of Inniskilling within a wreath	The Inniskillings (6th Dragoons) now forms part of 5th Royal Inniskilling Dragoon Guards
8th Regiment of Dragoons	VIII.D.	8th King's Royal Irish Hussars
10th Regiment of Dragoons	X.D.	10th Royal Hussars
14th Regiment of Dragoons	XIV.D.	14th Hussars now forms part of 14th/20th The King's Hussars
Buff and Black Facings		
2nd or Queen's Regiment of Dragoon Guards	Queen's Cypher within the Garter	The Queen's Bays
4th Regiment of Horse	IV.H.	7th Dragoon Guards now forms part of 4th/7th Royal Dragoon Guards
9th Regiment of Dragoons	IX.D.	9th Queen's Royal Lancers
11th Regiment of Dragoons	XI.D.	11th Hussars
White Facings		
3rd Regiment of Dragoon Guards	III.D.G.	3rd Dragoon Guards now forms part of 3rd Carabiniers
7th or the Queen's Regiment of Dragoons	Queen's Cypher within the Garter	7th Queen's Own Hussars
12th Regiment of Dragoons	XII.D.	12th Royal Lancers
2nd Regiment of Horse	II.H.	5th Dragoon Guards now forms part of 5th Royal Inniskilling Dragoon Guards
Green Facings		
4th Regiment of Dragoons	IV.D.	4th Queen's Own Hussars
13th Regiment of Dragoons	XIII.D.	13th Hussars now forms part of 13th/18th Royal Hussars

Another similar Royal Warrant was issued on 19th December, 1768, in which several further items, designed to achieve regimental distinction, were introduced, from which it may be assumed that those laid down in the 1751 Royal Warrant failed in this purpose. It will be seen from the following notes from the 1768 Warrant that the idea of distinctive badges had taken root. Normally, only items of general application are noted.

Cavalry

The Badge or Rank of the Regiment to be painted on the Bells of Arms.

Camp Colours to have the Rank of the Regiment in the centre.

The Number of the Regiment to be on the buttons, except in the three Regiments of Dragoon Guards, where the initials of the regimental title would be on the buttons, instead of the number.

Officers of Dragoon Guards, Horse and Dragoons to have an epaulette on the left shoulder, those of Light Dragoons to have one on each shoulder.

The first regiments of Light Dragoons were raised in 1759, that is, after the 1751 Warrant was issued. In the 1768 Warrant it is laid down that their coats are to be lapelled to the waist and to have an epaulette on each shoulder.

Privates of Horse Regiments to wear red shoulder-straps.

Farriers to wear a horse shoe on the fore part of their caps.

Forage or watering caps to be red and to have the Rank of the Regiment on them.

The shoulder belt was employed to mark the different branches of the Cavalry arm, thus:

(a) The breadth of those of Dragoon Guards, Horse and Dragoons to be four and a half inches, whilst those of Light Dragoons to be only two and a half inches.

(b) The Horse to have cross belts, Dragoon Guards and Dragoons to have only one belt, except 8th Dragoons who were to have cross belts (hence one of their nicknames—The Cross Belts).

In the "General View" a few more badges for wear on housings and holster caps, additional to those mentioned in the 1751 Warrant, were authorized. They are as follows:

3rd, or Prince of Wales's Dragoon Guards: The Feathers issuing out of a Coronet.

12th, or Prince of Wales's Light Dragoons: The Feathers issuing out of a Coronet.

15th, or King's Light Dragoons: King's Crest within the Garter.

16th, or Queen's Light Dragoons: Queen's Crest within the Garter.

Infantry

In this Royal Warrant of 1768, dealing with Grenadier Caps, it is laid down that: "The Caps of the Grenadiers to be of Black Bear-Skin. On the front the King's Crest of Silver plated metal on a black ground, with the motto 'Nec Aspera Terrent.' A Grenade on the back part with the Number of the Regiment on it."

In the preceding section of this Royal Warrant, dealing with "Drummers and Fifers Caps" it is stated that: "The Drummers and Fifers to have Black Bear-Skin Caps. On the front the King's Crest of Silver plated metal, on a Black Ground, with Trophies

22

of Colours and Drums. The Number of the Regiment on the back part, as also the badges, if entitled to any, as ordered for the Grenadiers."

This is the first occasion that metal badges are mentioned for headdresses. This Royal Warrant also authorized the "Number of the Regiment" to be placed on buttons, gorgets and pioneers' caps.

Regiments entitled to badges to have them engraved on gorgets and worn on drummers' caps.

42nd, or Royal Highlanders to have in the centre of their Colours the King's Cypher within the Garter, and Crown over it; under it, St. Andrew with the motto "Nemo me impune lacessit." In the three corners of the second Colour, the King's Cypher.

60th, or Royal Americans to have in the centre of their Colours the King's Cypher within the Garter, and Crown over it. In the three corners of the second Colour the King's Cypher and Crown.

An effective distinction between regiments at close quarters was that the lace on the coats was white, but carrying various coloured worms or stripes. The practice was introduced before 1768, but the Warrant confirmed it. This colour scheme is set out below:

Rank and Title of the Regiments	Colour of the Lace
Blue Facings	
1st, or the Royal Regiment	White, with a Blue Double Worm.
2nd, or the Queen's Royal Regiment	White, with a Blue Stripe.
4th, or the King's Own Regiment	White, with a Blue Stripe.
7th, or Royal Fusiliers	White, with a Blue Stripe.
8th, or King's Regiment	White, with a Blue and Yellow Stripe.
18th, or Royal Irish	White, with a Blue Stripe.

Rank and Title of the Regiments	Colour of the Lace
21st, or Royal North-Brit. Fusiliers	White, with a Blue Stripe.
23rd, or Royal Welch Fusiliers	White, with Red, Blue, and Yellow Stripes.
41st, or Invalids	Plain Button-Hole.
42nd, or Royal Highlanders	White, with a Red Stripe.
60th, or Royal Americans	White, with Two Blue Stripes.
Yellow Facings	
6th Regiment	White, with Yellow and Red Stripes.
9th Regiment	White, with Two Black Stripes.
10th Regiment	White, with a Blue Stripe.
12th Regiment	White, with Yellow, Crimson, and Black Stripes.
13th Regiment	White, with a Yellow Stripe.
15th Regiment	White, with a Yellow and Black Worm, and Red Stripe.
16th Regiment	White, with a Crimson Stripe.
20th Regiment	White, with a Red and a Black Stripe.
25th Regiment	White, with a Blue, Yellow, and Red Stripe.
26th Regiment	White, with One Blue, and Two Yellow Stripes.
28th Regiment	White, with One Yellow, and Two Black Stripes.
29th Regiment	White, with Two Blue, and One Yellow Stripe.
30th Regiment	White, with a Sky-Blue Stripe.
34th Regiment	White, with a Blue and Yellow Worm, and Red Stripe.
37th Regiment	White, with a Red and a Yellow Stripe.
38th Regiment	White, with Two Red, and One Yellow Stripe.
44th Regiment	White, with Blue, Yellow, and Black Stripes.
46th Regiment	White, with Red and Purple Worms.
57th Regiment	White, with a Black Stripe.
67th Regiment	White, with Yellow, Purple and Green Stripes.
Green Facings	White, with Two Red Stripes.
5th Regiment	White, with Two Red, and Two Green Stripes.
11th Regiment	
19th Regiment	White, with Two Stripes, Red and Green.
24th Regiment	White, with One Red and One Green Stripe.
36th Regiment	White, with One Red and One Green Stripe.
39th Regiment	White, with a Light Green Stripe.
45th Regiment	White, with a Green Stripe.
49th Regiment	White, with Two Red, and One Green Stripe.
51st Regiment	White, with a Green Worm Stripe.
54th Regiment	White, with a Green Stripe.

Rank and Title of the Regiments	Colour of the Lace
55th Regiment	White, with Two Green Stripes.
63rd Regiment	White, with a very small Green Stripe.
66th Regiment	White, with One Crimson and Green, and One Green Stripe.
68th Regiment	White, with Yellow and Black Stripes.
69th Regiment	White, with One Red, and Two Green Stripes.
Buff Facings	
3rd Regiment or the Buffs	White, with Yellow, Black, and Red Stripes.
24th Regiment	White, with a Blue and Red Worm, and Buff Stripe.
22nd Regiment	White, with One Blue, and One Red Stripe.
27th, or the Inniskilling Regiment	White, with One Blue, and One Red Stripe.
31st Regiment	White, with a Blue and Yellow Worm, and small Red Stripe.
40th Regiment	White, with a Red and a Black Stripe.
48th Regiment	White, with a Black and a Red Stripe.
52nd Regiment	White, with a Red Worm, and One Orange Stripe.
61st Regiment	White, with a Blue Stripe.
62nd Regiment	White, with Two Blue, and One Straw-Coloured Stripe.
White Facings	
17th Regiment	White, with Two Blue, and One Yellow Stripe.
32nd Regiment	White, with a Black Worm and a Black Stripe.
43rd Regiment	White, with a Red and a Black Stripe.
47th Regiment	White, with One Red, and Two Black Stripes.
65th Regiment	White, with a Red and Black Worm, and a Black Stripe.
Red Facings	
33rd Regiment	White, with a Red Stripe in the Middle.
53rd Regiment	White, with a Red Stripe.
56th Regiment	White, with a Pink-coloured Stripe.
59th Regiment	White, with a Red and Yellow Stripe.
Black Facings	
50th Regiment	White, with a Red Stripe.
58th Regiment	White, with a Red Stripe.
64th Regiment	White, with a Red and Black Stripe.
70th Regiment	White, with a Narrow Black Worm Stripe.
Orange Facings	
35th Regiment	White, with One Yellow Stripe.

The next official milestone in the evolution of badges would appear to be found in "Rules and Regulations for the Sword Exercises of the Cavalry," published on 1st December, 1796. In this work some of the illustrations depict a trooper of the 10th Light Dragoons (now Hussars) wearing the Prince of Wales's plume as a badge on the right side of his headdress. In an article by L. E. Buckell, Esq., in the *Journal of the Society for Army Historical Research* (Vol. XX, p. 72), it is shown that Light Cavalry wore metal badges in their headdress much earlier than 1796. Whether this was done with official sanction is not clear, but it does indicate a general trend towards the wearing of badges, and a number of regiments wore them on uniform, including the gorget, long before their general introduction.*

Badges and the "Number of the Regiment" were brought into prominence with the introduction of the shako† for British infantry in 1800.‡ This was announced by a General Order dated "Horse Guards, 24th February, 1800," signed by Harry Calvert, then Adjutant-General. On the front of the shako was a large metal plate bearing the Royal Cypher within the Garter upon a trophy of various arms, banners and trumpets: a Lion below the Garter and a Crown above. In the centre at the top of the shako was a cockade called the Hanoverian Cockade, made of black silk or *crêpe* for officers and tooled leather for other ranks, with plume above, white for Grenadier Companies,

---

* "At this period (1805) the Sphinx was, by Regimental Order, adopted as the badge to be worn on bonnets in place of a regimental button as heretofore." ("History of The Gordon Highlanders," by Lieut.-Colonel C. G. Gardyne, p. 139.)

There are a number of collections of badges worn before 1881, one such collection being in the museum of the Royal United Service Institution, Whitehall, London, S.W.1.

† "Shako" is derived from the Hungarian "shako," meaning a military cylindrical hat with a "cask," or peak, to shade the eyes.

‡ An excellent article on "The British Infantry Shako," by Alex R. Cattley, will be found in the *Journal of the Society for Army Historical Research*, Vol. XV, pp. 188-208.

dark green for Light Infantry Companies, and red and white (white uppermost) for Battalion Companies.

As far as badges and numbers were concerned, the General Order authorized the number of the regiment to be engraved on each side of the Lion, except that regiments "which are entitled to that Distinction His Majesty grants permission to bear their Badges in the centre of the Garter," thus displacing the Royal Cypher.* As previously mentioned, a number of regiments had been granted badges to be on Colours. "The Grenadiers . . . may if their Colonels choose it, bear the Grenade, in the same manner as regiments entitled to wear their Badges"— *i.e.*, in the centre of the Garter.

"All soldiers shall wear the button of their respective regiments in the centre of the Cockade, except the Grenadiers, who will use the Grenade."

A different pattern shako was authorized in 1811, but did not come into general use until 1812 and was worn during the latter part of the Peninsular War and campaigns of a few years later. The large metal plate of the original shako has now given place to a smaller shield-shaped plate surmounted by a Crown. In the centre was "GR" (the Royal Cypher), and below this the number of the regiment, except in those regiments authorized to bear badges and inscriptions on their Colours, who had a smaller "GR" with the badge and inscription below, and the number or title under it. The cockade and plume was borne on the left side, instead of in the front, and had the regimental button on it, except that Light Companies had a small silver bugle and Grenadier Companies a small gilt grenade. Although this was the standard type of plate there were several variations of it.

A major variation occurred in 1814 under a General Order of 28th December, 1814, wherein it was ordered that "the Caps

---

* This does not appear to have been strictly observed in some regiments where the number was placed above the Crown or on each side of the Crown or the Lion.

of Rifle and Light Infantry Corps, and Rifle and Light Infantry Companies of Regiments shall have a Bugle Horn with the Number of the Regiment below it, instead of the Brass plate worn by the rest of the Infantry."

The "Regency Shako" was authorized by a General Order of 10th August, 1815, and brought a number of changes from the previous pattern. The cockade and plume resumed their original position in the front of the shako. The plate is domed and circular in shape, within a circle of lace with a central crimson line running through it ; the whole surmounted by a Crown. The regimental badges, numbers and battle honours were on a plate, except in Light Infantry Regiments and Light Infantry Companies, who had a bugle on the plate. About 1822 modifications were made to the officers' shako and the domed circular plate in the centre gave place to an eight-pointed star with a Crown upon the uppermost point. It may have been this star that suggested some of the stars in present-day badges.

A further change in the pattern of the shako was authorized by a Horse Guards Circular Memorandum of 22nd December, 1828, and as far as badges, etc., were concerned the main altera- tions were: for the officers—the Hanoverian Cockade introduced in 1800 had disappeared; on the front was a large gilt universal star surmounted by a Crown, upon which were borne the badges, devices, etc., of regiments as on the previous pattern. The Royal Marines and Militia wore the same pattern shako. On the men's shako the star bore the number of the regiment only, except that those of the Light Infantry Regiments and Light Infantry Com- panies had a bugle also, and the Grenadier Companies the grenade.

Various other changes took place in the patterns of shako, and the central device on the front alternated between stars, a wreath and the Garter within a large laurel wreath, on all of which either the badges, numbers, devices, or some of the battle honours awarded to regiments were worn.

The shako was abolished by General Order 40 of May, 1878,

and the spiked cloth helmet introduced, but during its seventy-eight years of existence the shako had established the method of wearing badges, devices, etc., on headdress which was carried over to the helmet.

Militia Regiments seem to have had badges on their clothing and appointments from about the end of the eighteenth century or early part of the nineteenth century, and some of the badges adopted by the Regular battalions in 1881 were based upon those of their Militia battalions.*

In the Dress Regulations up to 1874 badges are described as "devices," but in the next Regulations, those of 1883, they are described as badges. These were the first Dress Regulations to be published after the great Infantry reorganization of 1881, whereby single-battalion Line Regiments were linked in pairs, each pair forming one regiment. At the end of these Regulations is a long schedule headed "Badges of Territorial Regiments" which details the description of badges to be worn on buttons, tunics, helmet-plates, waistplates and forage caps. Since then every regiment and corps has had a badge, or badges, assigned to it, the description being published for general information.

The following drawings illustrate the first metal badge to be worn on headdresses, that for Grenadier Caps, referred to on page 30 (*Fig.* 1), how the Star form of centre-plate evolved from the Shako-plate (*Figs.* 2-8) and the adoption of the Star form for the cloth helmet (*Fig.* 11). For headdresses that had a front so small that the original Star could not be accommodated, the device in the centre of the plate only was used, as shown in the Glengarry (*Fig.* 10), the Service Dress cap (*Fig.* 12) and the beret (*Fig.* 13).

Thus, the illustrations give a brief pictorial history of the development of badges on headdresses for nearly two centuries.

---

* An authoritative article on "English Militia Regiments, 1757-1935: their Badges and Buttons," by Major H. G. Parkyn, O.B.E., F.S.A., appears in the *Journal of the Society for Army Historical Research*, Vol. XV, pp. 216-248.

Fig. 1.   Grenadier Cap, 1776–83.   The front plate of universal type was made of white metal on a japanned ground.

Fig. 2.* 1800-12. Type, Officers. Badge-plate struck from a die all in one piece, officers in copper-gilt, other ranks in brass.

---

* This Shako and the six following illustrations have been reproduced by kind permission of The Society for Army Historical Research and Mr. A. R. Cattley, who drew all the illustrations (*Figs.* 1-13).

Fig. 3. 1812–16. Officers. Badge-plate in gilt for officers and brass for other ranks.   Regiments authorized to wear special badges and inscriptions on their Colours had a smaller "GR" with the badge and inscription below, and the Regimental number or title under all.

Fig. 4. 1816–22. Officers. The badge-plate is enclosed in a circle
of lace which has a central crimson line. For officers the plate was
usually in gilt and domed: regimental devices, battle honours,
etc., in gilt or silver or both, were mounted on the plate. For
other ranks the plate was in brass and bore the Regimental
number only.

Fig. 5. 1829-39. Men's. Badge-plate took the Star form and was made in brass. The officers' badge-plate was in the same form. The Crowned Star was of gilt but contained various devices, usually in gilt and silver.

Fig. 6. 1844-55. Officers. The "Albert Shako." A development of the Star form in Fig. 5. It is this form of plate that was adopted for the cloth helmet when introduced in 1878. (G.O. 4th May, 1878.)

Fig. 7. 1855-61. Quite a different type from the previous Shakos.
With a reduced height of front, consequently the Star ornament
is smaller than in the "Albert Shako" (Fig. 6). The shape of the
Shako was copied from the contemporary French pattern.

Fig. 8. The last Shako, 1869-78 (Officers). It will be noted that the Star pattern plate in Fig. 6 has given place to a different pattern.

Fig. 9. Fusilier Cap introduced in 1866.

Fig. 10.   Infantry Glengarry adopted in 1874.

Fig. 11.   Infantry Blue Cloth Helmet (Officer's home pattern).
Introduced 1878 (G.O. 40/1878.)   As this had a deep front the
badge plate was correspondingly deeper than in Figs. 7 and 8

Fig. 12.   Service Dress Cap.

Fig. 13.   Beret.

SOURCES OF DESIGN OF CAP BADGES

THERE ARE a few features common to many badges, such as the Crown which ensigns them, the encircling wreath, the title of the Regiment or Corps, either in full, abbreviated, or only the initial letters of the titles or, in the case of Cavalry, some figures. Excluding these general features, the components of badges have been taken from a considerable variety of subjects as shown below. In this table some regiments appear under more than one heading to indicate the source of their several features.

It may be thought that only Royal Regiments are permitted to embody a Crown in their badges, but that is not so, *vide* the badges of the following non-Royal Regiments which include the Crown—The Devonshire, The Suffolk and The East Lancashire Regiments and the Intelligence and Army Catering Corps. Conversely, not all Royal Regiments include the Crown in their badges, *vide* The Royal Scots, The Queen's, The Buffs (Royal East Kent Regiment), The King's Own and The Royal Northumberland Fusiliers.

ROYAL REGALIA AND ARMS

Features, Items, etc.	Regiment or Corps	Page
Royal Cypher	The Life Guards	57
	Royal Horse Guards	59
	Royal Horse Artillery	149
	Royal Engineers	153
	Royal Army Service Corps	308
	Norfolk Yeomanry	141
	Military Provost Staff Corps	319
	Duke of York's School	336
	Corps of Royal Military Police	315
	Royal Military Academy Sandhurst	334
Royal Crest	15th/19th Hussars	80
	The Loyal Regiment	224
	Parachute Regiment	253

ORDERS OF KNIGHTHOOD

PERSONAL ARMS

Features, Items, etc.	Regiment or Corps	Page
Warwick Family Bear	Warwickshire Yeomanry	96
Hamilton Family Star	The Cameronians	195
Duke of Wellington's Crest and Motto	The Duke of Wellington's Regiment	204
Stafford Family Knot	The South Staffordshire Regiment	212
	The North Staffordshire Regiment	239
	Staffordshire Yeomanry	99
Seaforth Family—Stag's Head and Motto	The Seaforth Highlanders	243
Gordon Family—Stag's Head and Motto and Coronet	The Gordon Highlanders	244
Argyll Family—Boar's Head; and Sutherland Family—Cat	The Argyll and Sutherland Highlanders	248
Sutherland—Cat	5th Bn. Seaforth Highlanders	277
Swan of Dukes of Buckingham	The Buckinghamshire Bn. Oxfordshire and Buckinghamshire Light Infantry	273
	Royal Bucks Hussars	128
Beaufort—Portcullis	Royal Gloucestershire Hussars	110
Lord Rolle—Crest	Royal Devon Yeomanry	133
Clan Fraser—Stag's Head	Lovat Scouts	146

CIVIC ARMS

Features, Items, etc.	Regiment or Corps	Page
Army Badge	General Service Corps	327
White Horse of Kent	The Queen's Own Royal West Kent Regiment	231
	569 Searchlight Regiment (Royal West Kent)	300
	Kent Yeomanry	125
Essex Arms	Essex Yeomanry	145
Cambridge Castle	Cambridgeshire Regiment	259
Bury St. Edmunds Castle	The Loyal Suffolk Hussars	134
Castle and Motto of Exeter	The Devonshire Regiment	174
Castle of Guildford	The East Surrey Regiment	202
Castle and Mottoes of Edinburgh	The King's Own Scottish Borderers	193

ARMOUR, WEAPONS, ETC.

46

Features, Items, etc.	Regiment or Corps	Page
Gun (continued)	568th S/L. Regt., R.A. (St. Pancras)	299
Machine Gun	Small Arms School Corps	318
Tank	Royal Tank Regiment	91
	42nd Bn. Royal Tank Regiment	303
Grenade	Grenadier Guards	155
	The Royal Northumberland Fusiliers	166
	The Royal Fusiliers	168
	The Lancashire Fusiliers	186
	The Royal Scots Fusiliers	187
	The Royal Welch Fusiliers	189
	The Royal Inniskilling Fusiliers	196
	The Royal Irish Fusiliers	247
Lance	9th Lancers	73
	12th Lancers	76
	16th/5th Lancers	82
	24th Lancers	87
	27th Lancers	90
	Royal Army Educational Corps	320
Sword	25th Dragoons	88
	Royal Army Dental Corps	321
	Army Physical Training Corps	325
Rifle	Royal Pioneer Corps	322
	Small Arms School Corps	318
Carbine	3rd Carabiniers	63
	3rd/4th Co. of London Yeomanry	116
	Hampshire Yeomanry	127
Shovel and Pick	Royal Pioneer Corps	322
Parachute	Parachute Regiment	253
Carisbrooke Castle	8th Bn. The Royal Hampshire Regiment	270
Claymore	Highland Regiment	256
Kris	Malay Regiment	344
Spear	Reconnaissance Corps	92

BATTLE HONOURS

Features, Items, etc.	Regiment or Corps	Page
"Waterloo"	The Royal Scots Greys	68
	The Rifle Brigade	249
"Jellalabad"	The Somerset Light Infantry	176
"Hindoostan"	The Royal Leicestershire Regiment	183

47

MYTHOLOGY, ETC.

MUSICAL INSTRUMENTS

ANIMALS

Features, Items, etc.	Regiment or Corps	Page
Lamb	The Queen's Royal Regiment	163
	6th (Bermondsey) Bn. The Queen's Royal Regiment	302
	622 H.A.A. Regt., R.A. (Queen's)	304
Stag	The Sherwood Foresters	222
Hart	The Bedfordshire and Hertfordshire Regiment	181
	The Hertfordshire Regiment	260
	Herts Yeomanry	130
Tiger	The Royal Leicestershire Regiment	183
	The Royal Hampshire Regiment	210
	The York and Lancaster Regiment	240
	Malay Regiment	344
Elephant	27th Lancers	90
	The Highland Light Infantry	242
Horse	R.E.M.E. (see under Civic Arms)	
	Berkshire Yeomanry	131
Lions	The Cyprus Regiment	345
	The Herefordshire Regiment	261
Lioness	W.R.A.C.	331
Camel	Sudan Defence Force	343
Fox	East Riding of Yorkshire Yeomanry	118

BIRDS

Features, Items, etc.	Regiment or Corps	Page
Eagle	The Royal Dragoons	67
	The Royal Scots Greys	68
	Army Air Corps	251
	Glider Pilot Regiment	251

FRUIT, FLOWERS, WREATHS, ETC.

Features, Items, etc.	Regiment or Corps	Page
Leek	Welsh Guards	160
Rose	Derbyshire Yeomanry	109
	Hampshire Yeomanry	127
	The Royal Fusiliers	168
	The East Yorkshire Regiment	179
	The Green Howards	184
	The East Lancashire Regiment	201

RELIGION

GENERAL

BACKING TO BADGES

LETTERING

ROMAN NUMERALS

MATERIALS OF WHICH BADGES ARE MADE

BADGES ARE made of various materials, gilt, gilding metal, silver, silver plate, chromium plate, bronze, and, during the late war, plastic; some are now embroidered.

With a view to conserving metal during the late war, plastic badges were introduced in December, 1941, for a limited number of Corps, but in June, 1942, this was extended to the whole of the Army, except in the case of those badges where production in plastic was impracticable.

At the present time a number of badges are being altered, so it is possible that the statement herein that a badge is made of a certain metal will not be up to date. This aspect of badges can only be correctly stated when the design of badges becomes stabilized. In future all officers' badges, normally made in silver, will be in silver plate.

Generally speaking, the badges of other ranks are made in metal to correspond to those of officers of the same regiment or corps—*i.e.*, where officers' badges are made of silver or silver plate, other ranks' are made in white metal; or where officers' badges are in gilt, those for other ranks are in gilding metal. For this reason no mention is made of the metals of which other ranks' badges are made in several instances in the following pages.

The Royal Cypher (GR VI) pierced, within a circle inscribed "The Life Guards", and crown above the circle. Officers' badges in Service dress cap are made in bright bronze and those of other ranks are in gilding metal.

Life Guards and Royal Horse Guards.—Officers of both regiments wear exactly the same badge in their No. 1 Cap, viz., the Royal Cypher within the Garter with crown above, all in gilt: background to Royal Cypher in red enamel.

FROM ITS inception in 1660 as individual Troops this regiment has always been closely associated with the Sovereign and, accordingly, its badges have had a Royal character.

When Charles II was in exile he formed a Troop of Life Guards from his loyal followers about 1658, and this later became the King's Troop. A second Troop, the Duke of York's, was also formed during Charles's exile. The third Troop was formed in 1659 by George Monk, later Duke of Albemarle, when Commander-in-Chief of the Commonwealth Forces. A fourth Troop was raised in Scotland in 1661, after Charles's Restoration. Horse Grenadiers were added in 1679. A reorganization took place in 1788, resulting in the regimentation of the existing Troops as the 1st and 2nd Regiment of the Life Guards respectively. In 1922 these two regiments were amalgamated to form the present regiment.

The Royal Cypher (GR VI) pierced, within a circle inscribed "Royal Horse Guards", and crown above the circle. Officers' badges in Service dress cap are made in bright bronze and those of other ranks are in gilding metal.

RAISED IN 1661 under the Colonelcy of the Earl of Oxford, its duties have been closely associated with the Sovereign, hence the Royal character of its badge. It was not, however, until 1827 that the Royal Horse Guards were placed upon the same footing as The Life Guards in regard to privileges enjoyed by Household Cavalry.

When William of Orange came to England in 1688 he brought with him some Dutch Horse Guards who wore blue coats like Oxford's regiment. To distinguish the latter it was popularly referred to as "The Oxford Blues," and although the Dutch Horse Guards returned to Holland soon after the Revolution, this soubriquet continued to be used. Lord Oxford ceased to be Colonel of the Regiment in 1668 and his name was gradually dropped from association with "The Blues," but "The Blues" was eventually officially incorporated into the official title.

ROYAL ARMOURED CORPS
GENERAL

A mailed gauntlet for the right hand, fist clenched, palm to the front, with a billet on the wrist inscribed "RAC"; issuing from the wrist upwards, two concentric circles, barbed; the whole ensigned with the Imperial Crown. Officers' badges are made in silver plate; other ranks' badges are made in white metal.

THE ROYAL ARMOURED CORPS was formed in April, 1939, by grouping together a number of existing Regiments of Cavalry of the Line that had been mechanized and the Royal Tank Regiment. Later, the remaining Regiments of Cavalry of the Line and some Territorial Army regiments were added, and in December, 1940, and January, 1941, the newly raised regiments of Dragoons, Hussars and Lancers were also included.

The armoured fist in the badge is symbolic of the hard punch the R.A.C. give the enemy, and the concentric circles with arrow-heads represent pincer movements.

Each individual regiment of the R.A.C. has its own badge, but the badge depicted above is worn by recruits at training regiments or awaiting posting to units, and officer cadets who have never served with an R.A.C. regiment (other than a training regiment).

This badge depicts the double-headed Eagle from the Arms of the late Emperor Francis Joseph II of Austria. Officers' badges are made in silver plate and other ranks' in white metal.

THE REASON for the adoption of this badge is that the late Emperor was Colonel-in-Chief of the Regiment from 1896 until the outbreak of the Great War, 1914-1918. The wearing of this badge ceased in 1915, but was resumed in 1937.

Before the adoption of the Eagle the regiment had as its badge the Royal Cypher within the Garter.

This regiment has been a Royal Regiment from the time it was raised in 1685 by James II at the time of the rebellion headed by the Duke of Monmouth. Its title then was "2nd, or Queen's Regiment of Horse." In 1714, there being no Queen Consort to George I, the title was changed to "The King's Own Regiment of Horse." A further change took place in 1746 on conversion to Dragoons, when its title became "1st, or King's Regiment of Dragoon Guards" ("Guards" was added to indicate its previous superior status as Horse).

THE QUEEN'S BAYS (2ND DRAGOON GUARDS)

The word 𝕭𝕬𝖄𝕾 *in Old English script within a wreath of laurel with the Imperial Crown between the ends of the wreath. The officers' badges are made in gilt or gilding metal and the other ranks' in gilding metal.*

THE WORD 𝕭𝕬𝖄𝕾 originated as a nickname for the regiment. About the middle of the eighteenth century it was mounted on bay-coloured horses, a practice which was long maintained. So fixed had this soubriquet become that the regiment was universally identified by it, and in 1870 the word 𝕭𝕬𝖄𝕾 was incorporated into the official regimental title.

The wreath is officially described as laurel, but is of bay leaves, bay belonging to the laurel family.

The regiment was raised as the 3rd Horse in 1685 at the time of the Monmouth rebellion and became "The Princess of Wales's Own Regiment of Horse". in 1715. On the accession of George II in 1727 the Princess became Queen Consort and the regiment's title was accordingly altered to "The Queen's Own Royal Regiment of Horse." On conversion to Dragoons in 1746 the title became "2nd, or Queen's Regiment of Dragoon Guards."

3RD CARABINIERS (PRINCE OF WALES'S DRAGOON GUARDS)

A pair of crossed carbines, muzzles uppermost, on the cross of the carbines the Prince of Wales's plume and motto, and on the butts of the carbines a scroll inscribed "3rd Carabiniers". For officers' badges the coronet from which the plume issues, and the scroll, are in gilt; the plume, motto and carbines are in silver plate. For other ranks the badge is in gilding metal and white metal.

THE 3RD DRAGOON GUARDS were raised in 1685 as Horse, being converted to Dragoon Guards in 1746 and granted the title "Prince of Wales's" in 1765. The Carabiniers (6th Dragoon Guards) were also raised in 1685 as Horse, being granted the title of "Carabiniers" in 1691 by William III for service in Ireland. Converted to Dragoon Guards in 1788. These two regiments were amalgamated in 1922.

The Prince of Wales's plume in the badge emphasizes the honour title of the 3rd Dragoon Guards, whilst the crossed carbines perform the same function for the Carabiniers. The title scroll inscription links both regiments.

An eight-pointed star, thereon a circle inscribed "Quis Separabit—MCMXXII"; within the circle, St. George's Cross with the Princess Royal's Coronet superimposed thereon. For officers the badge is in silver with St. George's Cross on a background of red enamel; for other ranks the badge is in gilding metal.

THE DESIGN of the badge is based, mainly, on the Star of the Most Illustrious Order of St. Patrick, incorporating the Cross of St. George from the Most Noble Order of the Garter. The Roman numerals "MCMXXII" refer to the year in which the two regiments were amalgamated—1922—to form the present regiment (see below). The coronet of the Princess Royal, which occupies the central position in the badge, links the regiment with the honour title "Princess Royal's," granted to the 7th in 1788 (see below).

The 4th was raised as Horse in 1685 and served many years in Ireland. In 1788 it was converted to Dragoon Guards and designated "4th Royal Irish Dragoon Guards," "Royal Irish" being granted in recognition of its long and faithful service in Ireland.

The 7th were raised in 1688 as Horse and served in Ireland about the middle of the eighteenth century. In 1788 it too was converted to Dragoon Guards, being granted the title "7th Princess Royal's Dragoon Guards" in honour of the then Princess Royal, H.R.H. Princess Charlotte Augusta Matilda, eldest daughter of George III, hence the Princess Royal's coronet in the badge.

The 4th and 7th were amalgamated in 1922 to form one regiment, being designated the "4th/7th Dragoon Guards," but in 1936 the title "Royal" was conferred upon it.

5TH ROYAL INNISKILLING DRAGOON GUARDS

The monogram "VDG" surmounted by a crown. For officers and other ranks the badge is in white metal.

THE COMPOSITION of this badge is merely the regimental title reduced to its briefest form. It does not suggest any of the historic associations of the two regiments, amalgamated in 1922, which wear it.

The 5th were raised in 1685 as Horse, being converted to Dragoon Guards in 1788. In 1804 they were granted the honour title of "Princess Charlotte of Wales's."

The Inniskillings (6th Dragoons) were raised from members of the Horse Regiments which defended Enniskillen when besieged by King James in 1688. They were brought on to the permanent establishment as a Dragoon regiment on 1st January, 1689.

In 1922 these two regiments, one Dragoon Guards and the other Dragoons, were amalgamated under the title "5th/6th Dragoons," this being altered in 1927 to "5th Inniskilling Dragoon Guards"; "Royal" was granted in 1935 at the time of George V's Silver Jubilee.

In October, 1948, a new design of cap and collar badge was approved, being an Eagle with outstretched wings, standing on a bar; below the bar, a tablet inscribed with the Arabic numeral "105"; a laurel wreath rests upon the Eagle's breast. For officers the badge is in gilt and silver plate; and for other ranks in gilding and white metal.

AT THE battle of Waterloo (18th June, 1815), Captain Clarke of the regiment saw the standard-bearer of the French 105th Infantry Regiment trying to hide his standard. Clarke rode straight for him and compelled him to relinquish the standard, which was caught by Corporal Stiles, who bore it away in triumph. In commemoration of this exploit the regiment was granted the badge of the Eagle.

Captain Clarke later became Lieutenant-General Sir Alexander Kennedy Clarke-Kennedy, and Corporal Stiles received a Commission in the West India Regiment.

THE ROYAL SCOTS GREYS
(2ND DRAGOONS)

An Eagle in silver plate, with a wreath round its neck, standing on a tablet inscribed "Waterloo" also in silver plate; below the Eagle, a scroll inscribed "Royal Scots Greys" in gilt. The officers' badge is described; other ranks have the same badge in corresponding metals.

AT THE battle of Waterloo on 18th June, 1815, when the great Duke of Wellington defeated Napoleon, the Royal North British Dragoons, as this regiment was then designated, was the Scottish element in the famous Union Brigade. Sergeant Charles Ewart of the regiment, with great intrepidity, attacked the standard-bearer of the French 45th Regiment and captured the flag, which was surmounted by an Eagle. In commemoration of this brilliant exploit the regiment has adopted the Eagle as the main device of its badge.

The White Horse in galloping action on a tablet representing the ground; below, a scroll inscribed "3rd The King's Own Hussars". For officers the White Horse and ground are in silver plate and the scroll is in gilt; for other ranks the corresponding metals are white metal and gilding metal.

THIS WAS one of the regiments of Dragoons raised by James II in 1685 at the time of the rebellion led by the Duke of Monmouth. Its first Colonel was Charles, Duke of Somerset, and in recognition of his services as Lord-Lieutenant of Somerset in command of the county Militia during the rebellion, the regiment was honoured with the title of "The Queen Consort's Regiment of Dragoons." When George I came to the throne in 1714 there was no Queen Consort so the title was altered to "The King's Own," and by 1742 the regiment was numbered the "3rd," and in 1861 it was converted to Hussars, hence the title on the scroll.

Under the Royal Warrant for Clothing of 19th December, 1768, the regiment was authorized to wear the badge of the White Horse within the Garter on its second and third guidons, housings and holster-caps. In time the badge was adopted for wear on clothing.

F

A circle inscribed "Queen's Own Hussars" with a spray of laurel in the centre of the bottom of the circle; within the circle the Roman numeral "IV" ornamented. Above the circle the Imperial Crown and below the circle a scroll inscribed with the motto "Mente et Manu" (With might and main). For officers the circle and crown above are in gilt, and the Roman numeral "IV" and motto scroll below the circle are in silver plate, and for other ranks the corresponding metals are gilding and white metals.

THIS REGIMENT was raised in 1685 as Princess Anne of Denmark's Regiment of Dragoons. By 1742 it was numbered the "4th," and by the Adjutant-General's letter of 23rd June, 1788, was granted the Royal title of "Queen's Own." In 1818 it was converted to Light Dragoons, and in 1861 to Hussars, hence "IV Queen's Own Hussars."

The motto "Mente et Manu" was granted under Army Order 157 of 1906.

The Rt. Hon. Winston Churchill served in this regiment and has been Colonel of the Regiment since 22nd October, 1941.

A circle inscribed "7th Queen's Own Hussars"; within the circle, the monogram "QO" reversed and intertwined; the Imperial Crown above all. The whole of the badge is in gilding metal with the exception of the monogram, which is in silver plate. The officers' badge is described: other ranks have the same corresponding metals.

THIS REGIMENT was formed in 1690 in Scotland as Dragoons. Disbanded in 1714, it was restored to the army the following year and under the Secretary of War's letter of 1st August, 1715, was granted the title "H.R.H. The Princess of Wales's Own Regiment of Dragoons." On the accession of the Prince of Wales as George II, the Princess of Wales became Queen Consort and the regimental title was accordingly altered to "The Queen's Own Dragoons." By 1742 it was numbered the "7th." It was converted to Light Dragoons in 1783 and to Hussars on 25th December, 1807, hence the title in the circle and the monogram "QO."

8TH KING'S ROYAL IRISH HUSSARS

Officers' badge is a harp surmounted by Royal Crest in silver plate; below harp, Roman numeral "VIII" in gilt; below all, a scroll bearing the motto "Pristinae virtutis Memores" (Mindful of our former valour) in gilt. Other ranks' badge as depicted above: a harp, with a winged female figure forming part of the composition, with the Imperial Crown above and resting on the wing, and below the harp a scroll inscribed "8th King's Royal Irish Hussars." The harp is in white metal and the crown and scroll are in gilding metal.

WILLIAM III raised this regiment as Dragoons in 1693 from among "known Protestants" in Ireland, to replace another Dragoon regiment that he had sent to Flanders during his war in the Low Countries against France. By 1742 it was numbered the "8th," and on 25th December, 1775, became Light Dragoons. Two years later it was granted the Royal title of "King's Royal Irish," and on 21st September, 1822, was converted to Hussars.

Its country of origin is therefore commemorated by the Irish Harp in the badge and the word "Irish" in its title. Its conversion to Hussars is also commemorated in the scroll on the badge.

A pair of crossed lances with pennons flying outwards; on the cross of the lances the Arabic figure "9"; within the upper portion of the crossed lances and above the figure "9", the Imperial Crown; embracing and resting on the lower portion of the crossed lances, a scroll inscribed "Lancers". For officers all in silver plate: for other ranks, in white metal.

TO MEET the rebellion led by James Stuart, the Old Pretender, in 1715, George I raised a number of Dragoon regiments in July, 1715: the senior of these was the regiment under the Colonelcy of Major-General Owen Wynne. By 1742 it was numbered the "9th," and in 1783 was converted to Light Dragoons. Under *London Gazette* notice of 5th October, 1816, the regiment was ordered to be armed and equipped as Lancers, but it was not until July, 1830, that its title was changed to "9th (or Queen's Royal) Regiment of (Light) Dragoons (Lancers)." The Royal title was in honour of Queen Adelaide, Consort of William IV. The present form of the title was adopted in 1920.

10TH ROYAL HUSSARS
(PRINCE OF WALES'S OWN)

The three feathers of the Prince of Wales's plume issuing from the coronet; the motto "Ich Dien" (I serve) inscribed on scrolls on each side of the coronet; below all, a scroll inscribed "10th Royal Hussars". Officers—plume and motto in silver plate, coronet and title scroll in gilt. Other ranks in corresponding metals.

LIKE THE previous regiment, the 10th Hussars were also raised in July, 1715, as Dragoons, by George I to meet the rebellion led by the Old Pretender. By 1742 it was numbered the "10th," and in 1783 was converted to Light Dragoons. At this time, by the Adjutant-General's letter of 29th September, 1783, it was granted the title of "10th, or Prince of Wales's Own Light Dragoons." H.R.H. The Prince of Wales, afterwards George IV (1820-1830), was appointed Colonel of the regiment on 18th July, 1796. This accounts for "Prince of Wales's Own" in the regimental title and the Prince of Wales's plume, coronet and motto in the badge. In March, 1811, the title became "10th (or Prince of Wales's Own Royal) Regiment of (Light) Dragoons (Hussars)."

The crest of the late Prince Consort, Prince Albert of Saxe-Coburg-Gotha, with a scroll below inscribed with his motto, "Treu und Fest" (Faithful and Firm). The badge is in gilt for officers and in gilding metal for other ranks.

RAISED AS Dragoons in 1715, the regiment was converted to Light Dragoons in 1783 and to Hussars in 1840.

When Prince Albert came to England in 1840 for his marriage to Queen Victoria, the 11th Light Dragoons furnished an escort to him from Dover to Canterbury. In commemoration of this service the regiment was converted to Hussars and had conferred upon it the royal title of "11th (or Prince Albert's Own) Hussars," which in 1920 assumed its present form.

Prince Albert was appointed Colonel of the regiment on 30th April, 1840. He died at Windsor Castle on 14th December, 1861. The regiment wears no badge in the beret.

12TH ROYAL LANCERS (PRINCE OF WALES'S)

A pair of crossed lances with pennons flying outwards; on the cross of the lances, the Prince of Wales's plume, coronet and motto "Ich Dien" (I serve); above the Prince of Wales's plume and within the upper portion of the crossed lances, the Imperial Crown; below the Prince of Wales's plume and within the lower portion of the crossed lances, the Roman numeral "XII". For officers the three feathers of the plume, the motto and lower half of each pennon are in silver plate, the remainder of the badge being in gilt. For other ranks the corresponding metals are white metal and gilding metal.

THIS REGIMENT was also raised as Dragoons in July, 1715, to meet the rebellion led by the Old Pretender. By 1742 it was numbered the "12th," and in 1768 was converted to Light Dragoons and granted the title "12th, or Prince of Wales's Light Dragoons."

Owing to the fine performance of the French Lancer regiments at the battle of Waterloo on 18th June, 1815, some British Light Dragoon regiments were converted to Lancer regiments, and this regiment was so converted in 1816, and at the same time was granted the title "Royal."

The Prince of Wales's plume therefore represents the honour title granted in 1768, the Roman numeral is the number it has borne for over two hundred years, and the crossed lances epitomize its role since 1816 until it became an armoured car regiment in 1928.

13TH/18TH ROYAL HUSSARS
(QUEEN MARY'S OWN)

The monogram "QMO," superimposed upon which is a scroll in the shape of the letter "Z"; the top arm of the scroll rests upon the top of the monogram and is inscribed with the Roman numeral "XIII"; the lower arm of the scroll supports the bottom of the monogram and is inscribed with the Roman numeral "XVIII"; the diagonal of the scroll joins the right end of the top scroll with the left end of the bottom scroll and is inscribed "Royal Hussars". The whole is ensigned with the Crown. The whole of the badge is in gilt for officers, other ranks gilding metal.

THE 13TH WERE raised as Dragoons in July, 1715, converted to Light Dragoons in 1783 and to Hussars in 1861. The 18th were raised as Hussars in 1858.

The 13th and 18th were amalgamated in 1922, hence the double figures in its title and on the scroll of the badge.

In 1910 the 18th were granted the Royal title of "Queen Mary's Own" on the accession of George V, which accounts for the monogram in the badge.

The Prussian Eagle in black japanned metal for officers and gilding metal for other ranks.

THE 14TH WAS raised as Dragoons in July, 1715, converted to Light Dragoons in 1776 and to Hussars in 1861. The 20th was raised as the 2nd Bengal Light Cavalry, converted to Light Dragoons in 1861 and to Hussars the following year.

The 14th and 20th Hussars were amalgamated in 1922.

The Eagle badge is connected with the 14th. In 1798 it was granted the title "14th (or Duchess of York's Own) Light Dragoons" in honour of Frederica Charlotte Ulrica Catherina, Princess Royal of Prussia, who married the Duke of York in 1791. The Prussian Eagle badge was adopted to commemorate this connection with the Prussian Royal House. It was worn until 1915, when it ceased, but was restored in 1931 as the badge of the amalgamated regiment.

15TH/19TH THE KING'S ROYAL HUSSARS

The Royal Crest within the Garter; attached to the lower portion of the Garter, the Roman numerals "XV" and "XIX"; the lower ends of the Roman numerals rest upon a scroll inscribed with the Regimental motto "Merebimur" (Let us be worthy). For officers the Garter and Roman numerals are in gilt, while the Royal Crest is in silver plate. The motto scroll and motto are in silver plate, but the groundwork of the motto is blue. For other ranks the corresponding metals are gilding and white metals.

THE 15TH WAS raised as Light Dragoons in 1759 under the Colonelcy of George Augustus Eliott, later Lord Heathfield, famous as the defender of Gibraltar during the great siege of 1779-1783. It was granted the title "The King's" in 1766 and was converted to Hussars in 1807. The 19th was raised in 1858 as the 1st Bengal Light Cavalry, became Light Dragoons in 1861 and Hussars in 1862.

The 15th and 19th Hussars were amalgamated in 1922.

The Royal Crest within the Garter was an old badge of the 15th, and the motto "Merebimur" also belonged to the 15th. The Royal elements of the regimental title are expressed in the badge, the Roman numerals of which express the historic regimental numbers.

A pair of crossed lances with pennons flying outward; on the cross of the lances, the Arabic number "16" resting on a scroll inscribed "The Queen's Lancers"; within the upper portion of the lances, the Imperial Crown. For officers the whole is in gilt, with the exception of the figure "16", the scroll and the lower half of each pennon, which are in silver plate. Other ranks, gilding metal and white metal.

THE 16TH WAS raised as Light Dragoons in 1759, was granted the title "The Queen's" in 1766, and was converted to Lancers in 1816. The 5th were raised from the defenders of Enniskillen in 1689, but were disbanded for insubordination in 1799. The disbandment was cancelled in 1858 and the regiment was restored to the establishment as the 5th Royal Irish Dragoons and became Lancers the same year.

The 16th and 5th Lancers were amalgamated in 1922.

The principal distinctive features of the badge (the figure "16" and the scroll) belong to the 16th, whilst the Lances reflect the role of both until they became mechanized.

A pair of crossed bones with a skull (Death's Head) super-imposed thereon; resting on the ends of the lower portions of the crossed bones is a scroll inscribed "or Glory". The interpretation of the whole badge is "Death or glory." For officers whole of the badge is in silver plate and for other ranks in white metal.

THE 17TH WAS raised in 1759 as Light Dragoons, being converted to Lancers in 1822. The 21st was raised in 1858 as the 3rd Bengal Light Cavalry, became 21st Hussars in 1861 and Lancers in 1897 in recognition of its distinguished service at the battle of Khartoum during the Sudan Expedition.

There is a romantic touch about this badge. When Major-General James Wolfe, the hero of Quebec, lay dying in the moment of victory on 13th September, 1759, he requested that his friend, Colonel John Hale, be allowed to take the despatch concerning the battle to the King. This was done and when the King saw Hale he appointed him Colonel of a Light Dragoon regiment about to be raised—the 17th. It is said that Hale chose the "Death or Glory" badge out of respect for Wolfe.

Cap badge: The capital letter "D"; above it the Imperial Crown, within it the Roman numeral "XXII" and below it a scroll inscribed "Dragoons". Collar badge: The Castle of Enniskillen on an eight-pointed star; beneath the Castle, a scroll inscribed "XXII". Officers' badges are in bronze and other ranks' in white metal.

THIS REGIMENT was raised in December, 1940, and disbanded in June, 1948.

The cap-badge is merely the regimental title in symbolic form.

As regards the collar-badge, the 22nd Dragoons were formed from cadres from the 4th/7th Royal Dragoon Guards and the 5th Royal Inniskilling Dragoon Guards. The eight-pointed Star is from the badge of the 4th/7th, and the Castle is from the collar-badge of the 5th Royal Inniskilling Dragoon Guards. Both "parents" are therefore represented in the offspring.

A previous 22nd Regiment of the Cavalry arm was the 22nd Light Dragoons, raised in 1760 and disbanded six years later. Two others, raised respectively in 1779 and 1794, were of short duration. A fourth, raised in 1794 as the 25th Light Dragoons, renumbered 22nd in 1802, saw service in South Africa in 1796, in the Mahratta War in India in 1799, in Java and again in India. It was disbanded in 1819.

The latest regiment, whose badge is depicted above, had a distinguished record of service in 21 Army Group during operations in North-West Europe.

The capital letter "H" surmounted by the Imperial Crown; below the "H", a scroll inscribed "23rd Hussars". Officers' badges are in bronze; for other ranks the "H" is in white metal and the remainder in gilding metal.

THIS REGIMENT was raised in December, 1940, and disbanded in June, 1948.

The badge is the regimental title in symbolic form.

Three previous regiments in the Cavalry had borne the number 23. The first dated from 1781 and served in India, where it was renumbered the 19th Light Dragoons; the next was an Irish regiment which existed from 1794 to 1802; and the third was raised in 1795 as the 26th Light Dragoons, renumbered 23rd in 1803. It served in the West Indies and later, in 1801, in the campaign against the French in Egypt. In the Peninsular War it distinguished itself at Talavera on 27th-28th July, 1809. It was disbanded in 1817.

The latest regiment, whose badge is depicted above, gained its laurels in Operation "Overlord," in action at Caen, Falaise, Antwerp, in Germany, and others on "the way."

A circle inscribed on the lower portion "Lancers"; within the circle and extending to its outer rim, a pair of crossed lances with pennons flying outward; across the centre of the circle and in front of the cross of the lances, the Roman numeral "XXIV". The officers' badges are in bronze and other ranks' in white metal.

THIS REGIMENT was raised in December, 1940, and disbanded in June, 1948.

The badge is the regimental title in symbolic form.

The number 24 was borne by a Cavalry regiment from 1794 to 1802, the 24th Light Dragoons. It was an Irish corps, and on its helmets it bore the motto "Death or Glory," which has long been that of the 17th (now 17th/21st) Lancers. The 27th Light Dragoons were raised in 1795, but were renumbered as the 24th in 1802. It served in St. Domingo, in Cape Colony and in India. In India it served under Sir Arthur Wellesley, later the great Duke of Wellington, in the Mahratta War. For its services in India it was awarded the badge of an Elephant superscribed "Hindoostan." It was disbanded in 1819.

A pair of crossed swords, points uppermost; on the cross of the swords the Roman numeral "XXV"; above the numeral and on the upper part of the swords, the Imperial Crown; below the numeral, a scroll inscribed "25th Dragoons". Officers' badges are in bronze; for other ranks they are—-the swords in white metal and remainder in gilding metal.

THIS REGIMENT was raised in January, 1941, and was disbanded in June, 1948.

The badge is the regimental title in symbolic form with the swords denoting a Cavalry connection.

In 1802 a Cavalry regiment, the 29th Light Dragoons, was raised, being renumbered 25th in 1802. It served in St. Domingo and in Cape Colony. In India it served under Lord Lake, and was granted the badge of an Elephant superscribed with the word "Leswarree" for its services. The battle of Leswarree (or Laswarree) was fought on 1st November, 1803, during the Mahratta War. The regiment was disbanded in 1818.

The Prussian Eagle with scroll below inscribed "XXVI Hussars". Officers' badges are in bronze and other ranks' in white metal.

THIS REGIMENT was raised in January, 1941, and disbanded in June, 1948.

The original members of the regiment were supplied by the 14th/20th Hussars, which accounts for the similarity of the badges.

This regiment was raised in India and became part of the 255 Indian Tank Brigade in 1942, the Brigade belonging, originally, to the 32 Indian Armoured Division until early 1943, when on amalgamation with the 43 Indian Armoured Division, it became the 44 Indian Armoured Division. By December, 1943, the 26th Hussars had become unbrigaded, having been transferred to the Central India Command for special training.

*A pair of crossed lances with pennons flying outwards;
on the cross, an Elephant's head; above and within the
upper portions of the lances, the Imperial Crown; below
the Elephant's head, the figure "27". Officers' badges are
in bronze; for other ranks the Elephant's head and lower
part of the pennants are in white metal and the remainder
in gilding metal.*

THIS REGIMENT was raised in January, 1941, and disbanded in
June, 1948.

The Elephant's Head was granted to the 27th Light Dragoons
for services during the Mahratta War of 1803. A year later it
was renumbered 24th and was disbanded in 1819. The Elephant's
Head therefore links the two regiments numbered "27." The
remainder of the badge is symbolic of the regimental title.

Within a laurel wreath, surmounted by a crown, an early model Tank; on the bottom of the wreath a scroll inscribed "Fear Naught". The officers' badges are in silver plate and other ranks' in white metal.

UNDER ARMY ORDER 79 of March, 1917, a special badge—a Tank —was approved for wear on the right upper sleeve of all ranks of the Heavy Branch of the Machine Gun Corps (disbanded 1921). In July, 1917, the Heavy Branch broke away from the M.G.C. and was constituted the "Tank Corps," and the sleeve badge became the basis for the regimental badge. The motto "Fear Naught" was granted to the Corps in 1922.

In recognition of its services in the Great War of 1914-18 the Corps was granted "Royal," hence Royal Tank Corps. When the R.T.C. became part of the newly formed Royal Armoured Corps in April, 1939 (A.O. 58/1939), the title was altered to Royal Tank Regiment.

RECONNAISSANCE CORPS

A vertical spear, point uppermost, on each side forked lightning; on the bottom of the spear and lightning, a scroll inscribed "Reconnaissance Corps". In bronze for officers and gilding metal for other ranks.

THE RECONNAISSANCE CORPS was formed in January, 1941, and took precedence next below The Rifle Brigade. In December, 1943, it became a part of the Royal Armoured Corps and was disbanded in August, 1946.

Although the Reconnaissance Corps was the first corps to be designated as such, corps performing similar duties have existed for as long as the Army itself. The famous Light Division of the Peninsular War (1808-1814) and our regiments called "Rifles" and "Light Infantry" were bodies highly trained in reconnoitring duties. The badge represents an epitome of the duties of the Corps, which worked at great speed as the spearhead of a force.

Within a laurel wreath surmounted by a crown, four shields placed in the form of a cross with the bottom points touching in the centre, each shield bearing the Arms of one of the following Inns, viz., Lincoln's Inn at the top, Inner Temple on the right, Gray's Inn at the bottom and Middle Temple on the left; on the bottom of the wreath, a scroll inscribed "Inns of Court Regt." The Arms on the shields are: Lincoln's Inn—A number of mill-rinds; in the top left-hand corner (canton), a Lion rampant. Gray's Inn—A Griffin. Inner Temple—A Pegasus. Middle Temple—A St. George's Cross, the Paschal Lamb on the centre. The badge is in gilding metal.

THIS TERRITORIAL ARMY Regiment is composed of members of the legal community belonging to the four Inns.

The earliest body formed by the Inns of Court appears to have been about 1584. A Volunteer corps raised by the Inns was reviewed by George III in 1803, when he gave it the nickname "The Devil's Own" on being informed that it was composed of lawyers. In 1860 it became The Inns of Court Volunteers, and has been an officers' training corps ever since, training large numbers of officers for the Great War of 1914-1918 and the late war.

THE ROYAL WILTSHIRE YEOMANRY
(PRINCE OF WALES'S OWN)
ROYAL ARMOURED CORPS

*The Prince of Wales's plume, coronet and motto "Ich
Dien" (I serve). For officers the coronet is in gilding metal,
the remainder of the badge in silver plate; other ranks'
badges in corresponding metals.*

THE SENIOR regiment of Yeomanry dates its origin from a resolu-
tion passed at a meeting in Devizes in May, 1794, to raise a Corps
of Volunteer Cavalry.

In 1830 the Wiltshire Yeomanry received the special honour
of the prefix "Royal" for services rendered during the Machine
Riots. This was the first honorary and distinctive title ever to
be conferred on a Yeomanry Regiment.

The escort furnished to the Prince of Wales on his visit to
Savernake in 1863 was the first Yeomanry escort His Royal
Highness had ever had, and to commemorate this, as well as to
mark his appreciation of the efficiency of the Regiment, the
Prince gave permission for it to be styled thenceforth "The
Prince of Wales's Own Royal Regiment, The Wiltshire Yeo-
manry Cavalry." The present badge was then taken into use.

THE WARWICKSHIRE YEOMANRY
ROYAL ARMOURED CORPS

The Bear and Ragged Staff. Officers' badges are in silver and other ranks' in gilding metal.

WHEN THE Gentlemen and Yeomen of Warwickshire were formed in 1794, they adopted the "Bear and Ragged Staff" as their crest, and prints of 1801 clearly show this.

It was natural that this crest of the Warwick family should be adopted, as it was already in use by the Warwickshire Militia (Foot). These changed their badge to the antelope when The Warwickshire Regiment adopted it as their badge. The Yeomanry, however, continued to wear the bear.

The crest of the bear is believed to date from the days of Arthal, Earl of Warwick, who lived in the reign of King Givas (or Gwas), who took the animal for his sign.

A later Earl named Morvidus is reputed to have slain a giant with an ash tree, and he incorporated the ragged staff into his crest. It is still the crest of the Warwick family and part of the crest of the borough of Warwick.

THE YORKSHIRE HUSSARS
(ALEXANDRA, PRINCESS OF
WALES'S OWN)
ROYAL ARMOURED CORPS

The White Rose of York surmounted by the Prince of Wales's plume, coronet and motto "Ich Dien" (I serve). The coronet is in gilding metal; the remainder of the badge is white metal.

THIS REGIMENT was formed on 13th August, 1794, as the 2nd or Northern Regiment of West Riding Cavalry, and in consequence ranks third in order of precedence.

In 1819 the title was changed to that of The Yorkshire Hussars. Its additional title, that of Alexandra, Princess of Wales's Own, was conferred upon it to mark the occasion of Queen Victoria's Diamond Jubilee, when the regiment provided a detachment to take part in the Royal procession through London.

Its present badge of the White Rose was the badge of the Yorkist Kings.

NOTTINGHAMSHIRE (SHERWOOD RANGERS) YEOMANRY ROYAL ARMOURED CORPS

A horn with lanyard within a strap inscribed "Notts Sherwood Rangers Yeomanry" surmounted by a crown. The badge is in silver plate for officers and gilding metal for other ranks.

THIS REGIMENT dates from 9th August, 1794, when three Troops, those of Retford, Mansfield and Newark, were accepted.

With the exception of the Newark Troop it was disbanded but reaccepted 22nd June, 1802, but through the continuous service of the Newark Troop it dates from 1794, and is fourth in the official order of precedence.

It was regimented 27th May, 1828, as the Sherwood Rangers Yeomanry Cavalry.

A bugle or horn is traditionally associated with Forest Rangers, and no doubt is the reason for its incorporation in the badge.

THE STAFFORDSHIRE YEOMANRY
QUEEN'S OWN ROYAL REGIMENT
ROYAL ARMOURED CORPS

*Officers: The Stafford Knot within the Garter inscribed
"Honi soit qui mal y pense": below, a scroll inscribed
"Pro aris et focis" (For our altars and our hearths), the
whole surmounted by a crown. Other ranks: The Stafford
Knot surmounted by a crown. The officers' badge is in
bronze: other ranks' in gilding metal.*

THE STAFFORDSHIRE VOLUNTEER CAVALRY, as it was first known,
was raised on 4th July, 1794, and consisted originally of five
troops raised at Newcastle, Lichfield, Walsall, Stafford and
Leek. In 1798, however, it was organized on a complete regimental
system and the different troops were no longer independent.

In 1832 the regiment paraded at Shugborough Park for the
visit of the Duchess of Kent and the Princess Victoria, and in
June, 1838, the Queen conferred upon the regiment the title of
The Queen's Own Royal Regiment.

The knot was a badge of the de Stafford family, and has been
incorporated into the Arms of Staffordshire and Stafford.

THE SHROPSHIRE YEOMANRY
ROYAL ARMOURED CORPS

Three Leopards' faces within a strap inscribed "Shropshire Yeomanry" surmounted by a crown. The badge is in gilding metal.

THE THREE Leopards' faces are from the Arms of Shrewsbury, where they appear on the seal of the Corporation as early as the fifteenth century. It is probable that they were adopted from the Royal Arms which appeared on a thirteenth-century seal.

The regiment is one of those whose badge is admitted into the Army List, where it is described as "The Arms of the Shropshire County Council." These resemble the arms of Shrewsbury town, which were "Three Golden Leopards' Faces on a red shield."

During the war of 1939-1945 the regiment was converted into the 75th and 76th Medium Regiments, Royal Artillery, but on the reorganization of the Territorial Army after the war it became a unit of the Royal Armoured Corps.

AYRSHIRE (EARL OF CARRICK'S OWN) YEOMANRY
ROYAL ARMOURED CORPS

The crest of the Earl of Carrick (a Griffin, with lion's head, flaming tongue and eagle's wings) on a wreath; below, a scroll inscribed "Ayrshire Earl of Carrick's Own Yeomanry". The badge is in gilding metal.

THE TITLE "Earl of Carrick" was extant in the twelfth century, and Carrick was one of the seven earldoms (mentioned in the Charter of Scone, dated 1114) by whose sanction the King of Scotland governed. The Carrick territory covered much of South Ayrshire and part of the adjoining counties.

The title became a Royal one by the marriage of the heiress to the father of Robert the Bruce, who became King of Scotland after Bannockburn in 1314. The title descended to Robert's grandson, David II, and since then has been the hereditary title of the male heir to the Scottish throne.

It was last held by H.R.H. The Prince of Wales until he became King Edward VIII in 1936.

The title of "Earl of Carrick's Own" was granted under Army Order 94 of 1897.

CHESHIRE (EARL OF CHESTER'S)
YEOMANRY
ROYAL ARMOURED CORPS

The Prince of Wales's plume, coronet and motto "Ich Dien" above a scroll inscribed "Cheshire (Earl of Chester's) Yeomanry". The badge is in bronze.

THE REGIMENT was raised in 1797 by Sir John Fleming Leycester.

In 1803 the Prince of Wales granted permission for the regiment to use his crest as their badge, with the title of the "Earl of Chester's Regiment of Yeomanry Cavalry," which a few years later was amplified into "H.R.H. the Prince Regent's Regiment of Cheshire Yeomanry."

The present title was granted to the regiment under *London Gazette* notice of 26th January, 1849.

Earl of Chester is one of the titles of the Prince of Wales.

THE QUEEN'S OWN YORKSHIRE DRAGOONS
ROYAL ARMOURED CORPS

The Rose of York surmounted by a Royal Crown. The badge is in gilding metal.

AT A MEETING held at Pontefract in 1794, presided over by the Duke of Norfolk, it was decided to raise a mounted corps in the West Riding. The corps was designated the "First or Southern Regiment, West Riding Yeomanry Cavalry."

In 1844 Her Majesty Queen Victoria approved the title of the regiment being changed to the "First West York Yeomanry Cavalry" and in 1889 to the "Yorkshire Dragoons."

The regiment furnished part of the escort to Queen Victoria on the occasion of Her Majesty's visit to Sheffield in 1897, and in the same year Her Majesty conferred the title of "Queen's Own" on the regiment.

Under A.O. 222/1941 they became the 9th Bn. K.O.Y.L.I. but became a Regiment of the Royal Armoured Corps on the reorganization of the Territorial Army after the War.

The White Rose of York was the badge of the Yorkist Kings.

THE LEICESTERSHIRE YEOMANRY
(PRINCE ALBERT'S OWN)
ROYAL ARMOURED CORPS

The crest of the Prince Consort with a scroll above inscribed "Leicestershire" and a scroll below inscribed "Prince Albert's Own Yeo" and below this another scroll inscribed "South Africa 1900–02". The badge is in gilding metal.

THIS REGIMENT dates officially from 5th September, 1803, but it was actually accepted in May, 1794, and disbanded after the peace treaty was signed in Amiens in 1802, being re-raised on the renewal of the war in the following year.

The regiment was granted the title of "The Prince Albert's Own" in the *London Gazette* of 20th February, 1844, hence the badge.

The regiment contributed two companies to the Imperial Yeomanry in the South African War, the 7th which formed part of the 4th Battalion, and the 65th of the 17th Battalion, and in consequence bears on its badge a scroll inscribed "South Africa 1900–02."

A ten-pointed star, the topmost point displaced by a crown: in the centre a circle inscribed "Arma pacis fulcra" (Arms the mainstay of peace); within the circle the Royal Cypher (GR VI) with crown above. The badge is in white metal.

FORMED ON 2nd May, 1798, and disbanded in 1802, it was re-raised as Frome Troop, 13th August, 1803, and united in 1804 with East Mendip Corps to form the Frome and East Mendip Regiment of Yeomanry Cavalry, which in 1814 was designated North Somerset Yeomanry Cavalry.

The regiment was reorganized as Dragoons on the formation of the Territorial Force in 1908.

By A.O. 40/1943 they were converted to the Royal Corps of Signals and became Air Formation Signals, and under A.O. 44/1947 they became R.A.C., and in May of that year were re-formed as the Divisional Armoured Reconnaissance Regiment to the 16th Airborne Division.

DUKE OF LANCASTER'S OWN
YEOMANRY
ROYAL ARMOURED CORPS

A Rose within a wreath, laurel on left and oak on right; a scroll inscribed "Duke of Lancaster's Own", the whole ensigned with a ducal coronet. The badge is in gilding metal.

THE RED ROSE of Lancaster appears in the badge, as the Duchy of Lancaster is a Royal dukedom.

The Duke of Lancaster's Own Yeomanry date from 1819, but were in fact the successors of various corps of Cavalry Volunteers which had existed in the county for varying periods during the previous century.

Since 1834 the reigning Sovereign has always been Colonel-in-Chief of the regiment, which received its present guidon from His Majesty King Edward VII in July, 1909.

During the 1939-1945 war the regiment formed two regiments of Medium Artillery, the 77th and 78th.

A double-headed Eagle grasping a bell in its right claw, the whole surmounted by a crown; below, a scroll inscribed "Lanarkshire Yeomanry". The badge is in gilding metal.

THE BADGE is based upon the seal of the Royal Burgh of Lanark. An early fifteenth-century seal bears a double-headed Eagle, and the bell was added in the latter part of the sixteenth century. The bell is said to be that of St. Kentigern, who dropped his bell accidentally into the River Clyde near Lanark.

During the war of 1939-1945 the regiment was converted into two Field Regiments of Royal Artillery, the 155th and 156th. Of these the 155th, which served with the 11th Indian Division, was "lost" in Malaya.

On the reconstruction of the Territorial Army after the war it became a unit of the Royal Armoured Corps.

THE NORTHUMBERLAND HUSSARS
ROYAL ARMOURED CORPS

A circle inscribed "Northumberland Hussars" ensigned with a crown; within the circle a castle and below the circle a scroll inscribed "South Africa 1900-02". The badge is in gilding metal.

THE CASTLE in the badge is the Norman castle in the Arms of Newcastle-on-Tyne.

Raised in 1797 as the Newcastle Troop, but disbanded in 1802. Re-raised in 1819 as Northumberland and Newcastle Regiment of Yeomanry Cavalry.

The regiment furnished both the 14th and the 15th Companies of the 5th Battalion Imperial Yeomanry in the South African War and therefore carry the battle honour "South Africa 1900-02" on a scroll below the badge.

In February, 1940, the regiment was converted into the 102nd Light Anti-Aircraft/Anti-Tank Regiment, R.A., but in March, 1941, gave up the anti-aircraft role and became the 102nd Anti-Tank Regiment, with the exception of one battery which went to the 25th L.A.A. Regiment.

*A Rose within a laurel wreath surmounted by a crown;
on the laurel wreath scrolls inscribed "South Africa 1900-
1901"; below, a scroll inscribed "Derbyshire Yeomanry".
The officers' badge is in gilt with the laurel wreath in
silver. Other ranks' badge is in white metal.*

THE REGIMENT was raised in July, 1794, and renewed service
accepted in April, 1803; ordered to be disbanded in 1828, but
the Radbourne Troop continued to serve without pay. In 1830
this troop was augmented and placed on pay, and the regiment
dates officially from this later date.

It provided the 8th Company, 4th Battalion Imperial Yeomanry, in the South African War, and this is reflected in the
battle honour on the badge. It saw service in the First World
War in Gallipoli and Macedonia.

It was expanded into two regiments in the Second World War.

ROYAL GLOUCESTERSHIRE HUSSARS
ROYAL ARMOURED CORPS

The badge is the insignia of the Duke of Beaufort. A portcullis or with azure nails, chains or surmounted by a ducal coronet, and underneath a scroll in Beaufort blue inscribed "Royal Gloucestershire Hussars." Officers wear an embroidered badge as described above when wearing a beret. Other ranks' badge is gilding metal.

THE CONNECTION of the regiment with the Duke of Beaufort dates back to 1834, when the several independent troops then existing in the county formed themselves into one regiment and the command was offered to Henry Marquis of Worcester (the eldest son of the sixth Duke of Beaufort, who became the seventh Duke).

He was succeeded as Colonel of the Regiment by the eighth Duke in 1854.

The present Duke of Beaufort is Honorary Colonel of the Regiment.

LOTHIANS AND BORDER HORSE
YEOMANRY

ROYAL ARMOURED CORPS

*A Garb (the heraldic term for a sheaf of wheat). The badge
is in gilding metal.*

THE BADGE has always been associated with the regiment; it
appeared on the guidon of the Tranent troop of the East Lothians
Yeomanry Cavalry (1799-1825).

It symbolizes the farmlands of East Lothian, which have always
been the source of the strength of the regiment.

It may be remarked that both the Wauchope family of Niddry
and the Earls of Winton carry the "garb" in their Arms and
both originated in East Lothian.

THE QUEEN'S OWN ROYAL
GLASGOW YEOMANRY
ROYAL ARMOURED CORPS

The Crest of Scotland over a wreath of thistles. The badge is in gilding metal.

THE REGIMENT was raised in 1797, but disbanded in 1802 and re-raised in 1803.

It was again disbanded in 1814, but re-raised again in 1819; ordered to be disbanded in 1828, but retained for a period without pay. It was finally re-raised as Glasgow Yeomanry Cavalry in 1848.

In the following year the regiment provided the escort to Queen Victoria and the Prince Consort when they visited Glasgow, and in recognition they received Her Majesty's gracious permission to style themselves "The Queen's Own Royal Regiment of Glasgow Yeomanry."

Converted into a Field Artillery Regiment after the First World War, they subsequently became an Anti-Tank Regiment in 1938, and on the re-formation of the Territorial Army after the Second World War became a unit of the Royal Armoured Corps.

THE FIFE AND FORFAR YEOMANRY
ROYAL ARMOURED CORPS

*The County badge which is known as the "Thain of Fife."
The badge is in white metal.*

THE EARLIEST troop, the Kirkcaldy Troop, was accepted for service on 17th June, 1797, and renewed service on 21st December, 1802. This troop was amalgamated to the Fife Yeomanry Cavalry Regiment in 1803, but disbanded in 1828.

Re-raised as Fife Regiment of Yeomanry Cavalry in 1831, but disbanded in 1838. Re-raised as Fife Volunteer Mounted Rifles (later Light Horse) 7th June, 1860, and on 7th May, 1901, King Edward VII approved of amalgamation with Forfar Light Horse as the Fife and Forfar Imperial Yeomanry.

It fought in the South African War as the 20th Company of the 6th Battalion Imperial Yeomanry. After the First World War the regiment was converted to an armoured car unit of the Royal Tank Corps.

THE CITY OF LONDON YEOMANRY
(ROUGH RIDERS)
ROYAL ARMOURED CORPS

The Arms of the City of London within a circle inscribed "The City of London Yeomanry"; below, a scroll inscribed "Rough Riders"; the whole ensigned with a crown. Officers' badge in silver and other ranks white metal.

THERE WAS an earlier London Volunteer Cavalry Regiment during the Napoleonic wars. The Loyal Islington Troop was accepted for service 26th April, 1798; this later became the Loyal London Volunteer Cavalry and was disbanded in 1814.

The present regiment was, however, raised for service in the South African War, being the 20th Battalion of Imperial Yeomanry, and gained the battle honour "South Africa 1900-02."

During the First World War it fought first as cavalry and later as a machine-gun unit. After the First World War it was for a time a battery of Royal Horse Artillery, but was subsequently converted to a Light Anti-Aircraft Regiment, in which role it fought throughout the Second World War.

WESTMINSTER DRAGOONS
ROYAL ARMOURED CORPS

Officers: The Royal Crest (Lion and Crown). Other ranks: The Arms of the City of Westminster. The other ranks' badge is in white metal.

RAISED UNDER Army Order 175 of 1901 as 2nd County of London Imperial Yeomanry and granted the additional title of Westminster Dragoons under Army Order 5 of 1903, the regiment received a guidon from King Edward VII in June, 1909.

Officers wear the badge of the Old London and Westminster Light Horse formed in 1779 and disembodied in 1829. This badge consists of the Royal Crest, crown surmounted by a lion.

3RD/4TH COUNTY OF LONDON YEOMANRY (SHARPSHOOTERS) ROYAL ARMOURED CORPS

The badge is a circle inscribed "County of London Yeomanry" enclosing the letters "CLY" in front of a pair of crossed rifles; below is a scroll inscribed "Sharpshooters"; the whole ensigned with a crown. The badge is in gilding metal with the letters "CLY" in white metal.

DURING THE 1939-45 war the 3rd and 4th were separate units, and their badges had the arabic numerals 3 and 4 respectively in place of the letters "CLY." On the reorganization of the Territorial Army, the present regiment perpetuates both units and the above badge was taken into use.

It is of interest to note that the regimental colours of green, yellow and mauve were the racing colours of Lord Dunraven, who raised the regiment.

THE NORTHAMPTONSHIRE YEOMANRY
ROYAL ARMOURED CORPS

*The White Horse of Hanover. Two badges are depicted.
1st Northamptonshire Yeomanry with the White Horse
only. 2nd Northamptonshire Yeomanry—the White Horse
is enclosed in an oval inscribed "Northamptonshire Yeomanry." Both badges are in white metal.*

THE OFFICIAL badge of the Northamptonshire Yeomanry is that
of the 2nd Northamptonshire Yeomanry, but the 1st Northamptonshire Yeomanry have never worn this and have always worn
the "Horse" only.

The 2nd Northamptonshire Yeomanry, formed when the
Territorial Army was "doubled up" in 1939, was disbanded on
the conclusion of hostilities.

The 2nd Northamptonshire Yeomanry badge was designed
from the old Northamptonshire Imperial Yeomanry badge,
which was exactly the same except that the title in the oval was
"Northamptonshire Imperial Yeomanry."

The regiment was originally raised on 3rd May, 1794, but
disbanded in 1828. Re-raised as independent troops in 1830, the
last of which was disbanded in 1873.

The present regiment dates from 7th February, 1902.

THE EAST RIDING OF YORKSHIRE
YEOMANRY
ROYAL ARMOURED CORPS

A Fox in full cry; below, a scroll inscribed "Forrard". The fox is in gilding metal and the scroll in white metal.

THE BADGE was designed by Colonel T. G. Clitherow, D.S.O., T.D., D.L., and owes its origin to the fact that the regiment was formed in 1903 from the fox-hunting landowners and farmers of the East Riding of Yorkshire. The motto is part of the hunting term "Hark Forrard."

The regiment served in the First World War in Egypt and Palestine as cavalry and in France as a machine-gun unit.

When the Yeomanry was reorganized after this war the regiment became the 26th (E.R.Y.) Armoured Car Company, Royal Tank Corps.

In 1938 the regiment was expanded into a Divisional Cavalry Regiment (mechanized) and regained its regimental identity as the East Riding Yeomanry.

In the Second World War the regiment served with the B.E.F. in 1939-1940, and landed again in France with the first wave on D Day and fought for the remainder of the war in North-West Europe.

The Badge is an oval inscribed "Scottish Horse 1900" with scrolls below inscribed "South Africa 1900 1901 1902"; a wreath of juniper and bay encloses the oval: St. Andrew's Cross is superimposed on the oval, which is ensigned with a crown. The badge is in white metal.

THE REGIMENTAL badge originally consisted of the letters "Scottish Horse 1900" forming an oval on which a St. Andrew's Cross was superimposed.

After the signing of peace in the South African War, Lord Tullibardine was commissioned to recruit two regiments in Scotland to carry on the name and honours of his regiment.

They were to be trained as cavalry as a unit of the Imperial Yeomanry.

The oval of the badge was then surmounted by a crown and encircled in a wreath of bay leaves and juniper, the badge of the Murray clan, of which the Duke of Atholl is the head.

Below the oval was added a scroll bearing the battle honours gained by the original Scottish Horse in South Africa.

NORTH IRISH HORSE
ROYAL ARMOURED CORPS

The badge is the Irish Harp ensigned with a crown; below the harp, a scroll inscribed "North Irish Horse". The badge is in gilding metal.

THE OFFICIAL date of the raising of this regiment is 7th January, 1902. It was subsequently transferred to the Special Reserve.

It served throughout the First World War in France and Flanders. After the conclusion of hostilities it was not re-raised, and it was not until the Second World War that the regiment again became an active unit.

As a regiment of the Royal Armoured Corps it fought in North Africa and Italy. Early in 1944 fought in Italy as the spearhead to Canadian Infantry and adopted a silver maple leaf on the brigade insignia.

On the reorganization of the Territorial Army after the war, the North Irish Horse became part of the Royal Armoured Corps, T.A.

SOUTH NOTTINGHAMSHIRE
HUSSARS

PRESENT TITLE: 307TH FIELD REGIMENT, ROYAL ARTIL-
LERY (SOUTH NOTTINGHAMSHIRE HUSSARS YEOMANRY)
(ROYAL HORSE ARTILLERY), T.A., AND 350TH HEAVY
REGIMENT R.A. (SOUTH NOTTINGHAMSHIRE HUSSARS
YEOMANRY), T.A.

*A slip of oak with acorn.   For officers the badge is in silver
plate and in white metal for other ranks.*

THE BADGE is emblematic of the oak forests of Nottinghamshire.
The Standard presented to the regiment in 1795 bore as a badge
an oak tree with golden acorns.

The present badge was taken into use in 1898; previously the
badge was the monogram "SNYC" superimposed on two
crossed swords surmounted by a crown.

After the First World War the regiment became the 107th
Regiment, R.H.A. (South Nottinghamshire Hussars Yeomanry),
which later became the 107th Medium Regiment. Its second
line, formed on the doubling up of the Territorial Army as the
150th Regiment, R.H.A. (South Nottinghamshire Hussars Yeomanry), was converted in 1940 to the 150th Field Regiment.
The above are the present titles of these two regiments.

DENBIGHSHIRE YEOMANRY

*The Prince of Wales's plume, coronet and motto "Ich
Dien" above a scroll inscribed "C & D Yeo". The badge
is in white metal with the scroll in gilding metal.*

AS IS usual with Welsh regiments, the Prince of Wales's badge
is worn with the addition of the regiment's title.

Raised in May, 1795, as the Wrexham Troop, and renewed
service in 1802; was increased to three troops in 1803, and in
1820 to five troops and designated Denbighshire Yeomanry
Cavalry.

After the First World War it was converted into two batteries
of the 61st Caernarvon and Denbigh (Yeomanry) Medium Regiment, R.A., and on the doubling up of the Territorial Army in
1939 it also formed the 69th Medium Regiment, R.A.

It wore the Royal Artillery cap badge after its conversion
until 1949, when the present badge was adopted.

WESTMORLAND AND CUMBERLAND YEOMANRY

PRESENT TITLE: 251ST (WESTMORLAND AND CUMBER-LAND) FIELD REGIMENT, ROYAL ARTILLERY, T.A.

An oval within a laurel wreath inscribed "Westmorland & Cumberland Y"; within the oval three ears of wheat; the whole surmounted by a crown. The badge is in bronze.

THE UNIT now wears Royal Artillery badges.

The badge was designed by the second Earl of Lonsdale, who raised the unit in 1819. The three ears of wheat represent the close association which the Yeomanry had with the land in former days.

When raised its title was the Westmorland Yeomanry Cavalry, but the title was changed in 1843 to the Westmorland and Cumberland Yeomanry Cavalry.

After the First World War it was converted into 51st (Westmorland and Cumberland) Field Regiment, R.A. (two batteries), and also formed the 109th Field Regiment on the doubling up of the Territorial Army in March, 1939.

THE PEMBROKE YEOMANRY

PRESENT TITLE: 302 FIELD REGIMENT R.A. (PEMBROKE YEOMANRY), T.A.

The Prince of Wales's plume, coronet and motto "Ich Dien" above a scroll inscribed "Fishguard". The coronet and scroll are in gilding metal; the remainder of the badge is in white metal.

IN 1797 occurred the French invasion of Fishguard. They gained a footing beneath Trehowell, the alarm was sent out, and Lord Cawdor, Commandant of the Castlemartin Yeomanry, got his men together in the middle of the night. Early next day they were at Fishguard, and after a council of war the Yeomanry and other volunteer units went to meet the invader. Issues were not joined; the French surrendered to Lord Cawdor the following day.

In 1853 H.M. Queen Victoria graciously approved of the word "Fishguard" being borne on Standards and appointments of the regiment, this being the first battle honour carried by any volunteer unit of the British Army and the only one for service in the British Isles.

KENT YEOMANRY

PRESENT TITLE: 297TH (KENT YEOMANRY) LIGHT ANTI-
AIRCRAFT REGIMENT, ROYAL ARTILLERY, T.A.

*The badge depicted is the Regimental flash which is worn
on the left arm, consisting of the White Horse of Kent on
a black diamond.*

THE REGIMENT wears the Royal Artillery cap badge and collar
badges, but wears a brass shoulder title of the letters "KY" and
also a regimental button of flat brass, the design being the White
Horse of Kent standing on a scroll inscribed "Invicta" with the
letters "KY" below.

The Royal East Kent Yeomanry (The Duke of Connaught's
Own) (Mounted Rifles) and The West Kent Yeomanry (Queen's
Own) were amalgamated in 1920 on conversion to Royal
Artillery and formed the 97th Field Regiment. They also formed
the 143rd Field Regiment on the doubling up of the Territorial
Army in March, 1939.

Before the conversion the badge of the Royal East Kent
Yeomanry was the White Horse of Kent on a scroll reading

"Invicta" within the Garter; the whole surmounted by a crown, and under a scroll inscribed "Royal East Kent Mounted Rifles."

The West Kent Yeomanry badge was the White Horse of Kent on a scroll inscribed "Invicta," surmounted by a crown, and a scroll under inscribed "West Kent (Queen's Own) Yeomanry."

THE HAMPSHIRE CARABINIERS
YEOMANRY

PRESENT TITLE: 295TH HEAVY ANTI-AIRCRAFT REGIMENT,
ROYAL ARTILLERY (HAMPSHIRE CARABINIERS YEOMANRY),
T.A.

*The Hampshire Rose within an oval inscribed "Hampshire
Yeomanry" supported by crossed carbines, surmounted by
a crown below a scroll inscribed "Carabiniers". The badge
is in gilding metal.*

WHEN FIRST formed the regiment was dressed as Lancers, but in
1884 Colonel the Hon. H. G. H. Crichton, formerly of the
10th Hussars, was appointed to the command and the regiment
was converted into Carabiniers.

During the 1914-18 war the regiment became a battalion of
The Hampshire Regiment. In 1920 they became the 7th Hants
(Yeomanry) Army Field Brigade, R.F.A. (T.A.), one battery
only. In 1922 the title was changed to 95th (Hampshire Yeomanry) Field Brigade. Converted to an anti-aircraft role in 1937,
the title was changed to the 72nd Anti-Aircraft Regiment, R.A.
(T.A.).

ROYAL BUCKS HUSSARS

PRESENT TITLE: 299TH (ROYAL BUCKS YEOMANRY) FIELD
REGIMENT, ROYAL ARTILLERY. T.A.

*A circle inscribed "Yeomen of Bucks Strike Home";
within the circle a swan with a coronet round its neck.
The circle surmounted by a crown; a scroll under inscribed
"Royal Bucks Hussars". The officers' badge is in silver;
the other ranks' badge is in gilding metal.*

THE WHITE SWAN is from the Arms of the Stafford family, Dukes
of Buckingham.

The regiment was raised in May, 1794, and consisted of five
troops styled Bucks Armed Yeomanry.

On the expansion of the Yeomanry in 1803 there were three
regiments in Buckinghamshire; of these the North and South
Regiments were disbanded in 1828, but the Mid-Bucks continued
to serve without pay until 1830, when they were placed on pay.

The title Royal was granted in 1845.

Between the two World Wars it formed with the Berkshire
Yeomanry the 99th Field Regiment Royal Artillery (T.A.).

THE QUEEN'S OWN DORSET YEOMANRY

PRESENT TITLE: 341ST MEDIUM REGIMENT, ROYAL ARTILLERY (QUEEN'S OWN DORSET YEOMANRY)

The Garter ensigned with a crown; within the Garter "Q.O. Dorset Y," the word "Dorset" being borne on a scroll; the whole within a laurel wreath; on the wreath, scrolls inscribed "South Africa 1900 1901" and "The Great War". The badge is in bronze.

RAISED IN 1794 and disbanded in 1802, the regiment was re-raised in 1803 and disbanded in 1814.

Re-embodied in 1830, the regiment had the title "Queen's Own" conferred upon it in 1843.

The regiment was converted to Royal Artillery in 1922. In the official announcement of the conversion it was expressly stated that "The distinctive badges and buttons worn by the Regiment are to be retained."

In the Second World War it served as the 141st Queen's Own Dorset Yeomanry, Field Regiment, R.A.

THE HERTFORDSHIRE YEOMANRY

PRESENT TITLE: 286TH (HERTS YEOMANRY) FIELD REGI-
MENT, ROYAL ARTILLERY, T.A., AND 479TH HEAVY
ANTI-AIRCRAFT REGIMENT, ROYAL ARTILLERY (HERTS
YEOMANRY), T.A.

*A hart trippant on a ford (the County Crest of Hertford-
shire). The badge is in gilding metal.*

THE REGIMENT was formed originally in June, 1794, as independent
troops, disbanded in 1824 and re-raised in 1830. Designated
Hertfordshire Yeomanry Cavalry in 1872.

During the South African War the regiment provided the
42nd Company of the 12th Battalion Imperial Yeomanry.

It received its guidon from King Edward VII in June, 1909.

In the First World War it served in Gallipoli, Egypt and
Palestine.

After the 1914-18 war the Hertfordshire Yeomanry became part
of the 86th Field Brigade (afterwards Regiment), Royal Artillery.
In 1938 a cadre from this regiment formed the 79th Anti-Aircraft
Regiment, Royal Artillery. The above are their present-day
titles.

THE BERKSHIRE YEOMANRY

The White Horse of Berkshire above a scroll inscribed "Berkshire". The officers' badge is in silver; the other ranks' badge is in gilding metal.

THE CHALK figure which gives its name to the Vale of the White Horse lies 850 feet above sea-level on the side of the Berkshire Downs above Uffington.

It was at least 1,000 years old when the Romans came to Britain, and its origin is lost in the mists of antiquity. Monkish chronicles of A.D. 1100 show it was called White Horse Hill in those days. The White Horse was covered over during the war on the grounds that it helped to show from the air the location of Swindon.

The Star and Crescent from the seal of the borough of Hungerford was worn as a regimental badge until 1902, and was then worn as a collar-badge for all ranks until 1921. It is still worn by officers in mess dress.

1st COUNTY OF LONDON YEOMANRY (MIDDLESEX, DUKE OF CAMBRIDGE'S HUSSARS)

PRESENT TITLE: 16TH AIRBORNE DIVISIONAL SIGNAL REGIMENT, T.A.

An eight-pointed star, the topmost point displaced by a crown: in the centre a circle inscribed "Pro Aris et Focis" (For our altars and our hearths), "M.D.C.H." Within the circle the Royal Cypher. The badge is in gilding metal, with the crown and star in white metal.

WHEN FORMED in 1797 the regiment was designated the Uxbridge Yeomanry Cavalry, and the first regimental badge of which a record exists was the Arms of Middlesex, but some time after 1830 the present badge was adopted bearing the same motto and the Royal Cypher of the reigning sovereign.

In 1871 the title of the regiment was Middlesex Yeomanry Cavalry (Uxbridge), and in 1884 it became Middlesex (Duke of Cambridge's Hussars) Yeomanry Cavalry.

Since early in 1920 it has formed part of the Royal Corps of Signals, but the regimental badge has remained the same.

ROYAL DEVON YEOMANRY

*The crest of Lord Rolle within a circle inscribed "Royal
Devon Yeomanry Artillery" surmounted by the Royal
Crest (Lion and Crown). The badge is in silver plate for
officers and bronze for other ranks.*

THE CREST of Lord Rolle is particularly appropriate to the Royal
Devon Yeomanry, as both the Devon Yeomanry Regiments
were raised by him.

The Royal First Devonshire Yeomanry Hussars were raised in
1794 and the Royal North Devonshire Yeomanry Hussars in
1798.

These two regiments were amalgamated after the First World
War to form the 96th (Royal Devon Yeomanry) Field Regiment,
R.A., and also formed the 142nd Field Regiment on the doubling
up of the Territorial Army in 1939.

The present badge was finally approved on 18th December,
1924.

THE DUKE OF YORK'S OWN LOYAL SUFFOLK HUSSARS

PRESENT TITLE: 308TH (SUFFOLK YEOMANRY) ANTI-TANK REGIMENT, ROYAL ARTILLERY, T.A.

A Castle; below this the date 1793 and a scroll inscribed "Loyal Suffolk Hussars". The castle and date are in gilding metal and the scroll in white metal.

ENGLAND DECLARED war on France in February, 1793, and amongst the earliest Yeomanry troops raised were those in Suffolk which were regimented in August, 1793, as the Suffolk Light Dragoons with Headquarters at Bury St. Edmunds. This is reflected in the present badge of the regiment, which shows the Castle of Bury St. Edmunds and the date 1793.

In 1892 King George V, then Duke of York, became Honorary Colonel of the Regiment, and two years later the regiment was granted the additional title of The Duke of York's Own.

134

THE QUEEN'S OWN
WORCESTERSHIRE HUSSARS

PRESENT TITLE: 300TH ANTI-TANK REGIMENT, ROYAL
ARTILLERY (WORCESTERSHIRE YEOMANRY), T.A.

*Within a laurel wreath surmounted by a crown a sprig of
pear blossom; superimposed on the wreath, a scroll inscribed "Queen's Own Worcestershire Hussars". The pear
blossom is in white metal and the remainder of the badge
in gilding metal.*

THE WORCESTERSHIRE YEOMANRY adopted khaki service dress in
1900, and with it an all-brass badge of the pear blossom surrounded by a wreath. This continued in wear up to 1913, when
the pear blossom was changed to white metal.

The Archers of Worcestershire in the Hundred Years War
wore the badge of the pear tree on their jerkins, and the volunteers had a pear tree as their badge, and no doubt the Yeomanry
chose pear blossom as their badge to keep the association which
has existed between the armed forces of the county and the pear.

THE WEST SOMERSET YEOMANRY

PRESENT TITLE: 255TH MEDIUM REGIMENT, ROYAL
ARTILLERY (WEST SOMERSET YEOMANRY), T.A.

*The badge is the Wyvern, the emblem of the ancient Kings
of Wessex, within an oval inscribed "West Somerset
Yeomanry"; below, a scroll inscribed "S. Africa 1900–01".
The badge is in gilding metal.*

THE REGIMENT now wears the Royal Artillery cap badge.

The earliest troop of this regiment was the Bridgwater Troop,
commissioned in July, 1794, and formed with other troops into
the West Somerset Regiment of Yeomanry Cavalry in 1798.

The regiment served in the South African War as the 2nd
Company in the 7th Battalion Imperial Yeomanry and bear the
honour "South Africa 1900–01" as part of the badge.

The West Somerset Yeomanry was converted to form two
batteries of the 55th (Wessex) Army Field Brigade, R.A., after
the First World War.

They became the 55th Field Regiment, R.A. (Wessex), in
1938, and in March, 1939, on the doubling up of the Territorial
Army, also formed the 112th Field Regiment, R.A. (Wessex).

QUEEN'S OWN OXFORDSHIRE HUSSARS

PRESENT TITLE: 387TH FIELD REGIMENT, ROYAL ARTILLERY (OXFORDSHIRE YEOMANRY), T.A.

The Cypher "AR" of Queen Adelaide surmounted by a queen's crown; below, a scroll inscribed "Queen's Own Oxfordshire Hussars". The badge is in bronze.

ORIGINALLY RAISED in 1798 and in 1818 regimented to form the North-West (later 1st) Regiment of Oxfordshire Yeomanry Cavalry.

The badge was adopted in 1835 as a result of a visit of Queen Adelaide, the wife of William IV, to Oxford in that year.

The regiment furnished guards of honour to her, and in consequence the title "Queen's Own Royal Oxfordshire Yeomanry Cavalry" appears to have been conferred upon it (Royal, however, dropped out of the title). "Queen's Own Oxfordshire Hussars" was adopted in 1881.

The regiment was the first Yeomanry Regiment to go on active service in the First World War.

MONTGOMERYSHIRE YEOMANRY

*A Dragon; below, a scroll inscribed "M.Y." The badge
is in white metal.*

THE REGIMENT was raised in 1803 but disbanded in 1828. It was
re-raised in 1831.

For the South African War it provided the 31st and 49th
Squadrons attached to the 9th Battalion Imperial Yeomanry, and
in 1901 it raised two more squadrons, the 88th and 89th.

In the First World War it fought in Egypt and Palestine and
in France and Flanders in 1918.

After the war it was converted to form two companies of the
7th (Montgomeryshire) Battalion, The Royal Welch Fusiliers.

This regiment was subsequently converted into a regiment of
the Royal Artillery, and its present title is 636th Light Anti-
Aircraft Regiment, Royal Artillery (Royal Welch).

LANCASHIRE HUSSARS

PRESENT TITLE: 349TH LIGHT ANTI-AIRCRAFT REGIMENT,
ROYAL ARTILLERY, T.A.

The badge is the Red Rose of Lancaster; below, a scroll inscribed "Lancashire Hussars". The badge is in gilding metal.

THE RED ROSE of Lancaster was the badge of the Lancastrian Kings.

The earliest troop, the Bolton Troop, was accepted in 1798, and after renewing service in 1802 was disbanded in 1814.

The Furness Troop, formed in 1819, was in 1828 regimented with the Bolton and Wigan Troops as the Lancashire Regiment of Yeomanry Cavalry.

In 1900, with the Duke of Lancaster's Own Yeomanry, it formed the 32nd Company of the 2nd Battalion, and afterwards the 23rd and 77th Companies of the 8th Battalion Imperial Yeomanry. It was awarded the battle honour "South Africa 1900–02."

It saw service in France and Flanders in the First World War and was converted to a regiment of the R.H.A. on the reorganization of the Territorial Army in 1920.

THE SURREY YEOMANRY
(QUEEN MARY'S REGIMENT)

PRESENT TITLE: 298TH (SURREY YEOMANRY, QUEEN MARY'S) FIELD REGIMENT, ROYAL ARTILLERY, T.A.

Within the Garter surmounted by a crown, the cypher of Queen Mary; below, a scroll inscribed "Queen Mary's Regiment Surrey Yeomanry". The badge is in gilding metal with a red enamel background to the cypher and also between the top and bottom portion of the scroll.

THE SURREY REGIMENT of Yeomanry Cavalry was first raised in 1794 and disbanded in 1828. It was re-raised in 1831 but disbanded in 1848.

The present regiment came into being as a result of the South African War and dates from 1901.

After the 1914-18 war, Queen Mary's Regiment (Surrey Yeomanry) was converted with the Sussex Yeomanry to form the 98th (Surrey and Sussex Yeomanry, Queen Mary's) Field Regiment, Royal Artillery. With the reorganization of the Territorial Army in 1947, the Surrey and Sussex Yeomanry became two separate regiments.

THE NORFOLK YEOMANRY
THE KING'S OWN ROYAL REGIMENT

PRESENT TITLE: 389TH LIGHT ANTI-AIRCRAFT REGIMENT, ROYAL ARTILLERY (NORFOLK YEOMANRY), T.A.

The Royal Cypher ensigned with a crown. The badge is in gilding metal.

IN MAY, 1901, King Edward VII authorized the raising of a Yeomanry Cavalry regiment in Norfolk with the title of "The King's Own Norfolk Yeomanry."

The title was changed to "The King's Own Royal Regiment of Imperial Norfolk Yeomanry" under Army Order 2 of 1906, and King Edward VII became Colonel-in-Chief.

After the First World War it became, with the Suffolk Yeomanry, a Field Brigade R.A. and later an Anti-Tank Regiment.

The Norfolk Yeomanry element formed the 65th Anti-Tank Regiment when the Territorial Army was doubled in 1939.

SUSSEX YEOMANRY

*On a shield six martlets, the whole on an ornamental
ground surmounted by a crown; below, a scroll inscribed
"Sussex Yeomanry". The badge is in gilding metal.*

THE BADGE is that of the ancient Kingdom of the South Saxons.

The scroll at the foot of the badge was added to the other
ranks' badge in 1906.

Officers' badges and other ranks' prior to 1906 had no scroll.

Although the present regiment dates from 1901, previous
regiments of Yeomanry were raised in Sussex in 1794 (disbanded
in 1828) and in 1831 (disbanded in 1848).

After the First World War it was amalgamated with the Surrey
Yeomanry to form the 98th Field Regiment, R.A.

On the doubling up of the Territorial Army this regiment
also formed the 144th Field Regiment, and in January, 1940, the
74th Medium Regiment, R.A., was raised from the Surrey and
Sussex Yeomanry.

The Prince of Wales's plume and coronet; below, a scroll inscribed "Glamorgan Yeomanry". The scrolls which normally carry the motto "Ich Dien" are left blank. The coronet and bottom scroll are in gilding metal, the remainder of the badge in white metal.

IN 1919 the Glamorgan Yeomanry was converted to form the 324th (Glamorgan Yeomanry) Battery of the 81st Field Brigade, Royal Artillery, T.A. In November, 1938, consequent on the reorganization of the Royal Artillery into two-battery regiments, 324th Battery combined with 323rd Battery, Glamorgan R.H.A. Before the reorganization was completed the Territorial Army was doubled, and the old 324th Battery was expanded to form one battery in the new 81st Regiment and continued as a battery of that regiment throughout the war.

The present title of this regiment is the 281st (Welsh) Field Regiment, Royal Artillery, T.A.; but at the present time there is no mention of the Glamorgan Yeomanry in the title of the unit.

THE BEDFORDSHIRE YEOMANRY

PRESENT TITLE: 305TH MEDIUM REGIMENT (BEDFORD-SHIRE YEOMANRY), ROYAL ARTILLERY, T.A.

An eagle, surmounted by a coronet, on which is super-imposed a castle. The badge depicted is the collar badge. The eagle is in gilding metal and the castle in silver for officers and in gilding metal for other ranks.

THE REGIMENT wear the Royal Artillery cap badge.

The badge is taken from the common seal of the corporation of Bedford and dates from the fifteenth century. The eagle formed part of the Arms of the Beauchamp family, and the castle represents Bedford Castle which used to stand on the north bank of the River Ouse.

The regiment also wears Bedfordshire Yeomanry buttons. Crossed Lancers surmounted by a crown, with the letters "B Y" on either side.

THE ESSEX YEOMANRY

*Two badges are in use: The Essex County Arms sur-
rounded by a circle inscribed "Decus et Tutamen" (Honour
and Protection) and surmounted by a crown; worn on the
beret and coloured forage cap. The Essex County Arms
surrounded by a circle inscribed "Essex Yeomanry" and
surmounted by a crown; below, a scroll inscribed "Decus
et Tutamen"; worn on the service-dress (peaked) cap.
Both badges are in gilding metal.*

LIEUT.-COLONEL R. B. COLVIN, C.B., raised the Essex Imperial
Yeomanry and commanded the regiment from 1902 to 1910.
During this period the badge had his family motto, "Audacter
et Sincere." Afterwards it was changed to "Decus et Tutamen"
the original watchword of the West Essex Yeomanry, which was
in existence from 1830 till 1877.

THE LOVAT SCOUTS

PRESENT TITLE: 677TH MOUNTAIN REGIMENT, ROYAL
ARTILLERY (LOVAT SCOUTS), T.A.

*Within a strap inscribed "Je Suis Prest" (I am Ready) a
stag's head. The badge is in white metal.*

THE CREST and motto are those of the Clan Fraser, of which the
late Lord Lovat was chief. He raised the unit in the South
African War, and it fought in that and both world wars; but
after the Second World War it was formed as a squadron of
the Scottish Horse, R.A.C.

On 1st January, 1949, it was re-formed as a Mountain Regiment, R.A. It still retains its traditional dress of Scout bonnet,
badge and collar badges, but does wear Royal Artillery cloth
shoulder titles.

An old-fashioned muzzle-loading gun; above, a scroll inscribed with the motto "Ubique" (Everywhere) ensigned by a crown; below the gun the motto "Quo Fas et Gloria Ducunt" (Whither Right and Glory Lead). For officers the badge is in gilt and for other ranks in gilding metal.

THE GUN is the symbol for artillery of all kinds. As the R.A. was formed in 1716 under the old Board of Ordnance, whose arms included three old cannon, the gun is a reminder of the origin of the Royal Regiment. Both mottoes were granted to the R.A. by *London Gazette* notice of 10th July, 1832, and epitomize the universal nature of its service. The badge was adopted the following year.

Another well-known badge of the R.A. is a grenade of seven flames with a scroll below inscribed "Ubique."

Units of the R.A. do not carry Regimental Colours, and therefore battle honours are not awarded to them as is done in the case of Cavalry, R.A.C. and Infantry. They take part, however, in all military operations, and this universal service is epitomized in the motto "Ubique." Since 1925 "Honour Titles" have been awarded to R.A. units, which are the counterpart of battle honours and consist of the names of engagements or of campaigns, or of famous commanders of troops and batteries.*

---

*A full list will be found in "Military Customs," Chap. VII, Gale & Polden Ltd.

The badge worn in the beret by the Royal Horse Artillery differs from that worn by the rest of the Royal Artillery in that it is the Royal Cypher (GR VI) within the Garter surmounted by a crown; below the Garter, a scroll inscribed "Royal Horse Artillery". In gilt for officers and gilding metal for other ranks.

The previous badge, shown for the Royal Regiment of Artillery, is worn by the R.H.A. in the service-dress cap and coloured forage cap.

THE R.H.A. was formed in 1793, and in the following year one of its troops distinguished itself at Vaux when serving under the Duke of York. "The Chestnut Troop" has gained fame in a number of campaigns, particularly in the Peninsular War where it served under the command of Captain Hew Ross (later a Field-Marshal) in the Light Division. When the R.H.A. is on parade with its guns it takes the place of honour in the matter of precedence and marches at the head of the Household Cavalry.

Two badges are worn, viz.:

Artillery badge: An old-fashioned cannon, with a scroll above inscribed "H.A.C" and a scroll below inscribed with a motto of the Company, viz. "Arma pacis fulcra" (Arms, the mainstay of peace). Above the scroll inscribed "H.A.C" a crown. The officers' Artillery badge is bronze, and for other ranks it is in gilding metal.

Infantry badge: Grenade with "HAC" on the ball in monogram form. The officers' Infantry badge is gilt em-broidered with "HAC" in silver. For other ranks the badge is gilding metal.

THIS ANCIENT Corps was granted a Charter of Incorporation in 1537 by King Henry VIII. Originally it was a Guild of Archers and Handgunmen, and as a military organization is probably the oldest in the world with a continuous history. The artillery badge is an adaptation of that of the Royal Artillery.

In appearance the infantry badge is very similar to that worn in the Grenadier Guards and was, presumably, authorized by William IV when he authorized the Infantry of the H.A.C. to wear uniform similar to the Grenadier Guards.

An old-fashioned gun superimposed upon the Maltese Cross; below, a scroll inscribed "Tutela bellicæ virtutis" (Custodian of military prowess); the whole ensigned with the Crown. For officers' forage cap the Maltese Cross is in silver and the remainder in silver gilt; for other ranks' service dress the Maltese Cross is in white metal and the remainder in gilding metal. These badges were adopted in 1939.

THE BADGE is based upon that of the Royal Regiment of Artillery, of which the Royal Malta Artillery is an integral part. The motto refers to the great gallantry of the defenders of Malta in 1565 against the Turks, and later against the French in 1798. The R.M.A. is the guardian of the traditions which these defenders created by their valour.

The Royal Cypher within the Garter, the whole enclosed in a laurel wreath; above and resting upon the top of the Garter, a crown; below the Garter and resting upon the lower portion of the laurel wreath, a scroll inscribed "Royal Engineers". Officers: The Garter, motto, Royal Cypher, crown and scroll are in gilt and are raised above the laurel wreath. The laurel wreath is in silver plate.

Other ranks: In gilding metal and white metal.

THE R.E. was formed in 1717 from the old Board of Ordnance, but there is nothing in the badge to link it with its original body.

Like the R.A., the R.E. also wear as a badge a grenade, with nine flames (the grenade of the R.A. has seven flames).

The R.E. have also been granted the mottoes "Ubique" (Everywhere) and "Quo Fas et Gloria decunt" (Whither Right and Glory Lead) (*London Gazette*, 10th July, 1832).

ROYAL CORPS OF SIGNALS

In March, 1947, the following badge was approved for this Corps—the Figure of Mercury, holding a caduceus in his hand, poised on a globe, the globe being superimposed on a scroll inscribed "Certa Cito" (Swift and Sure); the whole ensigned with a crown. For officers the crown and scroll are in gilt and the remainder in silver plate. Other ranks' badges are in gilding metal and white metal.

IN ROMAN mythology Mercury was Jove's speedy messenger. The caduceus was the ancient herald's wand and a symbol of Mercury. The globe represents the universal nature of the service of the Royal Signals.

Before March, 1947, the badge was the Figure of Mercury with caduceus, within an oval band inscribed "Royal Corps of Signals." The globe upon which Mercury is poised is within the lowest portion of the oval band; a crown above the oval band.

The Corps was formed in 1920.

A grenade. For officers the badge is in gold embroidery and for other ranks the badges are: (1) Warrant Officers, Orderly Room Sergeants and Band Sergeants—Grenade in bronze; on the ball in silver the Royal Cypher interlaced and reversed with crown above. (2) Sergeants and Musicians—Grenade, with Royal Cypher and crown embossed on the ball, all in gilding metal. (3) Local Sergeants, Lance-Corporals, Guardsmen and Drummers—Grenade in gilding metal (plain ball).

FROM THE time this regiment was raised by Charles II until 1815 it was variously designated "Our Own Regiment of Guards," "Our First Regiment of Foot Guards," sometimes shortened to "1st Foot Guards."

At the battle of Waterloo, 18th June, 1815, the regiment particularly distinguished itself by overthrowing the grenadiers of Napoleon's Imperial Guard, a feat which is commemorated in its present title, published in the *London Gazette* of 29th

July, 1815 (No. 17045), which was thus: "H.R.H. (the Prince Regent) has been pleased to approve of the 1st Regiment of Foot Guards being made a Regiment of Grenadiers, and styled 'The 1st or Grenadier Regiment of Foot Guards,' in commemoration of their having defeated the Grenadiers of the French Imperial Guards upon this memorable occasion."

The grenade badge therefore harmonizes with the new title.

OFFICERS   OTHER RANKS

The Star of the Order of the Garter. For officers the badge is in silver plate, the Garter and motto on a blue ground, and the cross in red enamel. For other ranks the badges are: (1) Warrant Officers, Drum Majors, Orderly Room Sergeants and Band Sergeants—The Star of the Order of the Garter as for officers but of squarer design and not elongated as is that of the officers. (2) All other ranks not mentioned in (1) above wear the badge in gilding metal.

THIS REGIMENT was formed in 1650 as a unit of the Commonwealth New Model Army, its first Colonel being George Monk, later Duke of Albemarle. It is therefore the oldest regiment of Foot Guards.

To sever the regiment's connection with the New Model a ceremony was held on Tower Hill, London, on 14th February, 1661, where they laid down their arms as a sign of disbandment and took "them up again as entertained by His Majesty in service." At the same ceremony "they were immediately advanced to His Majesty's service as an Extraordinary Guard to His Royal Person" (From *Mercurius Publicus No. 7*, 14th-21st February, 1661).

*The Star of the Order of the Thistle. For officers the badge
is in silver plate, the circle, motto and centre being gilt.
For other ranks the badges are: (1) The Star of the Order
of St. Andrew in silver plate, except for the motto, circle
and thistle, which are in gilt, is worn by Warrant Officers.
(2) The Star in white metal and gilding metal is worn by
Colour Sergeants, Sergeants and Musicians. (3) Star in
all gilding metal is worn by Local Sergeants, Corporals,
Lance-Corporals and Guardsmen.*

AT HIS Restoration in 1660 Charles II authorized the raising of a
Regiment of Scottish Foot Guards, under the Colonelcy of the
Earl of Linlithgow, by Commission dated 23rd November, 1660.
The Star of the Order of the Thistle is therefore most appropriate
as a badge for this ancient Scottish regiment.

An earlier regiment of Guards in Scotland descended from
that raised in 1642 under Archibald, Marquis of Argyll, for
service in Northern Ireland, which in 1650 formed the basis of
a Life Guard of Foot for Prince Charles, later Charles II.

The Star of the Order of St. Patrick. For officers the badge is in silver plate, the motto "Quis Separabit" (Who shall separate us?), date "MDCCLXXXIII" (1783—when the Order was instituted), and circle in gilt on a blue enamel ground. (The mantle and ribbon of the Order are sky blue.) Within the circle the Shamrock is in green enamel over the red Cross of St. Patrick. For other ranks the badges are:
(1) Warrant Officers—In silver plate with gilt centre.
(2) Colour Sergeants and Guardsmen—In gilding metal.
(3) Pipers—Large and in white metal.

THE REGIMENT was formed under Army Order 77 of 1900 by Queen Victoria "to commemorate the bravery shown by the Irish Regiments in the operations in South Africa in the years 1899 and 1900."

As St. Patrick is the Patron Saint of Ireland, this badge is appropriate to the regiment.

WELSH GUARDS

A leek. The officers' badge is made of gold embroidery on black cloth; other ranks wear a leek in gilding metal.

THE LEEK is an ancient badge of Wales as shown in the passage from Shakespeare (*King Henry V*, Act IV, Scene 7), referring to the Battle of Agincourt, fought on St. Crispin's Day, 25th October, 1415. The conversation is between Henry V and Fluellen:—

"FLUELLEN: Your grandfather of famous memory, an 't please your Majesty, and your great-uncle Edward the Plack Prince of Wales, as I have read in the chronicles, fought a most prave pattle here in France.

"KING HENRY: They did, Fluellen.

"FLUELLEN: Your Majesty says very true. If your Majesties is remembered of it, the Welshmen did goot service in a garden where leeks did grow, wearing leeks in their Monmouth caps; which, Your Majesty knows, to this hour is an honourable padge of the service; and, I do believe, your Majesty takes no scorn to wear the leek upon Saint Tavy's Day.

"KING HENRY: I wear it for a memorable honour; for I am Welsh, you know, good countryman."

The Welsh Guards are therefore in good company in wearing the badge worn by King Henry V.

THE ROYAL SCOTS
(THE ROYAL REGIMENT)

OFFICERS   OTHER RANKS

For Officers—the Star of the Order of the Thistle. The star is in silver plate and the motto circle is in gilt or gilding metal: the thistle in the centre is in gilt or gilding metal on a green enamel ground. For other ranks the badge is also the Star of the Order of the Thistle, but with St. Andrew with Cross and scroll below inscribed "The Royal Scots" in the centre in white and gilding metal.

THE ROYAL SCOTS have an unbroken record of continuous service from 1633. By Royal Warrant dated 28th March, 1633, Charles I granted to Sir John Hepburn permission to raise in Scotland a regiment for French service. The actual Royal Warrant appears in the Register of the Privy Council of Scotland, 2nd Series, Vol. V, and forms part of the Proceedings of 24th April, 1633.

"Hepburn" was too difficult to pronounce in the French tongue, so his regiment was called "Le Regiment de Hebron." In 1572 some Scottish companies had gone to the Netherlands to assist them against the occupying Spanish forces, and being continually reinforced they developed into the famous Green Brigade in Swedish service, the remnants of which were later incorporated into Le Regiment de Hebron.

THE QUEEN'S ROYAL REGIMENT
(WEST SURREY)

*The Paschal Lamb.   The badge is in frosted gilt or gilding
metal for officers and gilding metal for other ranks.*

THIS REGIMENT was raised by the Earl of Peterborough in 1661
to garrison Tangier on the north-west coast of Africa, which
formed part of the dowry of Princess Catherine of Braganza,
Portugal, on becoming Queen Consort to Charles II.

The reason for the adoption of this badge by the regiment has
not been precisely established. In the Royal Warrant of 1st July,
1751, it is confirmed to the regiment, to be borne on its Colours
as its "ancient badge."

Sir Peter Lely's painting of Queen Catherine shows a lamb in
the foreground, a pet she may have favoured, which might link
her with the regiment raised as a consequence of her marriage
to Charles II.

THE BUFFS
(ROYAL EAST KENT REGIMENT)

A Dragon above a scroll inscribed "The Buffs". The badge is in silver plate for officers and gilding metal for other ranks.

DURING THE REIGN of Queen Elizabeth some Independent Companies went to the Netherlands to help the Dutch fight against Spain as in the case of The Royal Scots. These companies developed into regiments which were disbanded in 1665. In the same year Charles II raised The Buffs from among those which had been disbanded.

Why the Dragon was adopted as a badge has not been established beyond doubt. It was a supporter to the Arms of Queen Elizabeth, who sent the original Independent Companies to the Netherlands, and was also associated with the Netherlands owing to a dragon being taken from the mosque of St. Sophia in Constantinople during the Crusades and placed in the belfry of Bruges and later taken to Ghent—circumstances which may have influenced its choice as a regimental badge. As a Colour badge it was confirmed to The Buffs by Royal Warrant of 1st July, 1751, as its "ancient badge."

THE KING'S OWN ROYAL REGIMENT
(LANCASTER)

The Lion of England from the Royal Arms on a bar inscribed "The King's Own". The officers' badges are in silver plate and those for other ranks in gilding metal.

THE REGIMENT was raised in 1680 and it is believed that William III granted it the Lion. As its "ancient badge" it was confirmed to the regiment by the Royal Warrant of 1st July, 1751.

The title "The King's Own" has an interesting history. In 1684 the regimental title was "H.R.H. The Dutches of York and Albany's Regiment of Foot," but when the "Dutches" became Queen Consort in 1685 the title was altered to "The Queen's Regiment of Foot." With the accession of George I the title was again altered to "His Majesty's Own Regiment of Foot," usually abbreviated to "The King's Own."

THE ROYAL NORTHUMBERLAND
FUSILIERS

*A grenade; on the ball a circle inscribed "Quo Fata Vocant"
(Whither the Fates Call), within the circle St. George
killing the dragon. For officers the grenade is in gilt or
gilding metal, with the exception of the detail on the ball,
which is in silver plate. For other ranks the badge is in
gilding metal and white metal.*

EXACTLY WHEN St. George and the Dragon was adopted as a
regimental badge is uncertain; it was confirmed to the regiment
as its "ancient badge" by Royal Warrant of 1st July, 1751, to be
borne on Colours.

The badge of a grenade is common to all Fusilier Regiments,
each having a distinguishing device on the ball, in this instance
St. George and the Dragon within a circle inscribed "Quo Fata
Vocant." This motto was inscribed on the regimental "Order
of Merit" when instituted in 1767, and is mentioned in Queen's
Regulations of 1844.

THE ROYAL WARWICKSHIRE
REGIMENT

An Antelope with a coronet round its neck and a rope attached thereto which is draped towards the front, then over its back, falling to the near side; the antelope stands on a straight scroll, below which is a wavy scroll inscribed "Royal Warwickshire". For officers the antelope and scrolls are in silver plate and coronet and rope in gilt; for other ranks the badge is in gilding metal and white metal.

BY ROYAL WARRANT of 1st July, 1751, the antelope was confirmed to the regiment as its "ancient badge" to be borne on Colours. Traditionally, the badge is associated with service in Spain during the War of the Spanish Succession (1704-1711). The regiment maintains an Antelope as the living symbol of its badge.

The regiment was raised in 1673 for Dutch service, but came on to the English Establishment in 1688. In 1751 it was numbered the 6th Foot and in 1782 "1st Warwickshire" was added, thus "6th (or 1st Warwickshire) Foot." (The 24th Foot was the "2nd Warwickshire," now The South Wales Borderers.) The title "Royal" was granted in 1832, and in 1881 the designation became "The Royal Warwickshire Regiment."

THE ROYAL FUSILIERS
(CITY OF LONDON REGIMENT)

A grenade, on the ball of which is the Garter ensigned with the crown, and within the Garter a rose. The mass of flames is roughly triangular in shape and the crown rests upon the "neck" between the flames and the ball. The badge is in bronze for officers and gilding metal for other ranks. The grenade is common to all Fusilier regiments, the distinguishing feature on the ball in this case being the Rose within the Garter ensigned with a crown. "The Rose within the Garter and crown over it" was granted to the regiment as a Colour badge by Royal Warrant of 1st July, 1751.

THIS REGIMENT was raised in London in 1685 and incorporated two old Independent Companies that had been stationed in the Tower. Its original duties were as a protective force for the artillery. In one of the histories of the regiment it is stated:

"Probably one of the reasons the Regiment was granted the Royal and ancient badge of the rose within the Garter surmounted with a Crown was that many old cannon were cast with this royal badge upon them until the reign of Queen Anne. Cannon of this period may be seen at the Tower of London and the Rotunda at Woolwich." The writer therefore sees a connection between the early duties of the regiment and the badge.

Note.—The sealed pattern now has a petal of the rose uppermost, and not the division between two petals as depicted.

THE KING'S REGIMENT
(LIVERPOOL)

The White Horse of Hanover in a prancing attitude, its hind legs standing on a straight scroll, below the scroll a wavy scroll inscribed "King's" in Old English lettering. For officers the White Horse is in silver plate, the remainder being in gilt or gilding metal; for other ranks the corresponding portions are in white metal and gilding metal. The White Horse was granted as a Colour badge by Royal Warrant of 1st July, 1751. See Appendix 4 for an account of the possible origin of such grants.

THE ROYAL TITLE of "King's" has a more certain history. When the regiment was raised in 1685 it was designated "Princess Anne of Denmark's Regiment of Foot"; when the Princess became Queen Anne in 1702 the title was altered to "The Queen's Regiment of Foot." On the accession to the throne of George I in 1714 the title was again changed to "The King's Regiment of Foot," usually shortened to "The King's," hence the inscription on the wavy scroll.

The figure of Britannia holding a sprig of olive in her right hand; a trident in her left hand resting against her left shoulder; an oval shield bearing the Great Union rests against her left forearm; the whole resting upon a tablet. For officers the badge is in silver plate and for other ranks in gilding metal.

THE REASON for the adoption of Britannia as the regimental badge has not been precisely established. It is traditionally associated with the battle of Almanza in Spain in 1707, during the War of the Spanish Succession, and was granted for service at that action. It was officially confirmed to the regiment in 1799 as its "ancient badge."

In keeping with the badge, the Regimental March is "Rule, Britannia."

THE ROYAL LINCOLNSHIRE
REGIMENT

OFFICERS   OTHER RANKS

*Before July, 1948, the regimental badge was the Sphinx
resting on a tablet inscribed "Egypt" in Old English, with
a scroll below inscribed "Lincolnshire". In November,
1946 (Army Order 167 of 1946), the regiment was granted
the title "Royal" for past services. In consequence of this,
changes were made in the design of the regimental badges,
which are now as follows : For officers, a diamond-cut
eight-pointed star, thereon a circle inscribed "Royal
Lincolnshire Regiment", within the circle the Sphinx
over the word "Egypt". For other ranks, the Sphinx over
the word "Egypt", resting on a scroll inscribed "Royal
Lincolnshire Regiment". In the officers' badges the star
is in silver plate and the circle gilt, and the Sphinx is in
silver plate on a blue enamel ground. The other ranks'
badges are in gilding and white metal.*

THIS REGIMENT was raised in 1685 by James II at the time of the rebellion led by the Duke of Monmouth. In 1751 it was numbered the 10th Foot, "North Lincolnshire" being added to its designation in 1782. In 1881 the numbers in regimental titles were abolished and territorial designations substituted: at this time the regiment became "The Lincolnshire Regiment," and, as mentioned above, was granted "Royal" in 1946, hence "Royal Lincolnshire Regiment" on the scrolls of the badges.

The Sphinx superscribed "Egypt" was granted to the 10th Foot in July, 1802, for service against the French (see Appendix 3).

The Lincolnshire Militia had a Star background to their badge, which might be the origin of the Star in that of the Regular regiment.

An eight-pointed star, the uppermost point displaced by a crown; on the star a circle inscribed "The Devonshire Regiment". Within the circle the Castle of Exeter above a scroll inscribed with the motto "Semper Fidelis" (Always Faithful). For officers the star, castle and title circle are in silver plate and the remainder in gilt or gilding metal. For other ranks the badge is in gilding metal.

THE CASTLE OF EXETER with the motto "Semper Fidelis" was a badge worn by Devonshire Militia, and is said to commemorate the defence of the city by the county Trained Bands during the Civil Wars.

This regiment was raised in 1685 by Henry, Duke of Beaufort, for the suppression of the rebellion led by the Duke of Monmouth. It was numbered 11th Foot in 1747, to which "North Devonshire" was added in 1782. The 2nd Battalion wore a cockade, or rosette, of the Colours of The French Croix de Guerre above the cap badge for service at Chemin de Dames on 27th May, 1918, during the Great War, 1914-1918.

The Castle of Gibraltar, with a scroll above inscribed "Gibraltar", and a key depending from the centre of the base and turned to the left, within a circle inscribed "Montis Insignia Calpe", the whole within an oak-leaf wreath; above the circle a crown and below the circle a scroll inscribed "The Suffolk Regt." The badge is in silver plate (scroll in gilt) for officers and white metal (scroll in gilding metal) for other ranks. For the significance of the Castle and Key of Gibraltar see Appendix 2.

THE REGIMENT was raised in 1685 by James II at the time of the Monmouth Rebellion. It was numbered 12th Foot in 1751, "East Suffolk" being added in 1782. When numbers ceased to be used with regimental designations in 1881 it was then allotted the title "The Suffolk Regiment."

The wreath of oak-leaves is less common in regimental badges than those of laurel.

THE SOMERSET LIGHT INFANTRY
(PRINCE ALBERT'S)

A bugle horn (mouthpiece to the right) with the initials "PA" in ornamental lettering between the strings; above the bugle a mural crown superscribed "Jellalabad" on a scroll. The badge is in silver plate for officers and white metal for other ranks. The bugle forms part of the badge of all Rifle and Light Infantry regiments. (See Appendix 5.)

THE REGIMENT was raised in 1685, numbered 13th Foot in 1751, to which "1st Somersetshire" was added in 1782. In 1822 it was converted to "Light Infantry." During the 1st Afghan War (1839-1842) it achieved great fame by its magnificent defence of Jellalabad. In the *London Gazette* of 30th August, 1842, the War Office announced that Her Majesty the Queen had been graciously pleased to confer certain honours on the regiment in recognition of its distinguished gallantry displayed during the campaigns in Burma and Afghanistan. These honours took the form of granting a royal title—viz., "13th, or Prince Albert's Regiment of Light Infantry"—and its facings being changed from yellow to blue, and the grant of a mural crown superscribed "Jellalabad" as a badge "as a memorial of the fortitude, perseverance and enterprise evinced by that regiment, and the several corps which served during the blockade of Jellalabad."

Since 1920 the title has been "The Somerset Light Infantry (Prince Albert's)," the initials "PA" in the badge are those of Prince Albert.

THE WEST YORKSHIRE REGIMENT
(THE PRINCE OF WALES'S OWN)

The White Horse of Hanover in a galloping attitude on ground, below the ground a scroll inscribed "West Yorkshire". For officers the White Horse and ground are in silver plate and the scroll in gilt or gilding metal; for other ranks the badge is in white metal and gilding metal. (See Appendix 4 for an account of the White Horse.)

THE REGIMENT was raised in 1685 and numbered 14th Foot in 1751. In 1782 "Bedfordshire" was added, which changed to "Buckinghamshire" in 1809. In 1881 the title became "The West Yorkshire Regiment (The Prince of Wales's Own)," hence "West Yorkshire" on the badge scroll.

The regiment was raised in Kent by Sir Edward Hales, an ardent royalist, but the name of the county of its birth has never appeared in its title. Companies were raised at Canterbury, Sittingbourne and Rochester.

THE EAST YORKSHIRE REGIMENT
(THE DUKE OF YORK'S OWN)

An eight-pointed star with the White Rose of York in the centre, the rose encircled by a laurel wreath; below the star a scroll inscribed "East Yorkshire". For officers the star is in gilt or gilding metal and the rose in silver plate on a black enamel ground; for other ranks the badge is in white metal and gilding metal (but no black enamel ground for the rose).

THE REGIMENT was raised in 1685 by James II at the time of the Monmouth Rebellion, and in 1751 it was numbered the 15th Foot. In 1758 it fought under James Wolfe at Louisburg, and in the following year at Quebec. In memory of its association with Wolfe it now wears a black ground on its officers' badges.

The North Yorkshire and 1st West Yorkshire Militias had as their badge the White Rose within a wreath with a crown above, which might have suggested the laurel wreath in the badge of The East Yorkshire Regiment.

In 1782 "The Yorkshire, East Riding" was added to its regimental number, but when regimental titles were reorganized in

1881 the designation became "The East Yorkshire Regiment." To mark the Silver Jubilee of King George V, the secondary title of "The Duke of York's Own" was conferred, His Royal Highness, now George VI, having been Colonel-in-Chief of the regiment since 10th October, 1922.

The main structure of this badge seems to be based upon the Star of the Order of the Bath (without the lions and central device) superimposed upon the Star of the Order of the Garter; in the centre is the Garter and motto, within which is a Hart crossing a Ford; below all a scroll inscribed "Bedfordshire and Hertfordshire". The officers' badge is in silver plate, the centre being blue enamel, and the other ranks' in white metal.

HENRY, EARL OF DELORAINE, was Colonel of this regiment from 7th April, 1724, to 9th July, 1730. He was invested with the Order of the Bath when it was revived by George I in 1725, and the Maltese Cross in the badge is traditionally associated with him. The origin of the Garter Star and Garter as part of the badge has not been discovered. The Hart crossing a Ford was introduced into the badge in 1881. It had been the badge of the Hertford Militia, which became a battalion of The Bedfordshire Regiment at that time.

Raised in 1688, it was numbered the 16th Foot in 1751, "Buckinghamshire" being added in 1782. In 1809 "Buckinghamshire" gave place to "Bedfordshire," and in 1881 the title became "The Bedfordshire Regiment." In recognition of the fact that many men from Hertfordshire served in The Bedfordshire Regiment in the Great War, 1914-1918, "Hertfordshire" was incorporated into the title under Army Order 269 of 1919, hence "Bedfordshire & Hertfordshire" in the scroll below the badge.

THE ROYAL LEICESTERSHIRE
REGIMENT

*The Royal Tiger superscribed "Hindoostan" and a scroll
below inscribed "Royal Leicestershire". For officers the
tiger and ground are in gilt (scratch bright finish) and the
scrolls in silver plate; for other ranks the corresponding
metals are gilding metal and white metal.*

THE ROYAL TIGER superscribed "Hindoostan" was granted to the
17th Foot, now The Royal Leicestershire Regiment, for services
in India from 1804 to 1823 (*London Gazette*, 25th June, 1825).
The regiment was granted the title "Royal" in November, 1946,
in recognition of its past services (A.O. 167/1946).

THE GREEN HOWARDS (ALEXANDRA, PRINCESS OF WALES'S OWN YORKSHIRE REGIMENT)

The letter "A", cypher of the late Queen Alexandra, with "Alexandra" inscribed on the cross-bar of the cypher; combined with the cypher is the Dannebrog inscribed "1875" on the cross; inscribed on a scroll below "The Princess of Wales's Own Yorkshire Regt.", the word "Yorkshire" forming a straight base for the cypher; a rose in the centre of the scroll; the whole ensigned with a crown. The badge is in bronze for officers and gilding metal for other ranks.

New badge not yet published:
The letter "A", cypher of the late Queen Alexandra, thereon the Dannebrog inscribed "1875", surmounted by a crown; below, a scroll inscribed "The Green Howards"; all in silver plate.

THE DESIGN of the badge relates mainly to Queen Alexandra, whose cypher forms a prominent feature. Her Majesty was a Danish Princess (the eldest daughter of King Christian IX of Denmark), hence the Dannebrog, or Danes' Cross, the date 1875 being the year in which the regiment was granted the honour title of "Princess of Wales's Own," she having married the Prince of Wales (later Edward VII) in 1863. This design was approved in 1908.

THE DANISH CROSS (The Dannebrog—"The Strength of Denmark") has an interesting origin. King Waldemar fought a great battle with the Estonians in 1219, at the outset of which his army was on the point of being heavily defeated. The moment was critical, so Waldemar prayed to God for help. Immediately he saw a great White Cross in the sky on a blood-red ground. This he interpreted as a providential sign for him to renew the battle with the assurance of victory. He told his army of his vision, and with fortified strength they went forward to complete victory. Ever since then the White Cross on a red ground has been the blazon of the national flag of Denmark.

Raised in 1689 and numbered 19th Foot in 1751, "1st Yorkshire, North Riding" was added in 1782, and, as mentioned above, "Princess of Wales's Own" was granted in 1875. In 1881 the title became "The North Yorkshire Regiment (Princess of Wales's Own)," being altered a few weeks later to "The Princess of Wales's Own Yorkshire Regiment," hence the inscription on the scroll. The rose is the White Rose of York.

The present title of the regiment dates from 1920.

A grenade, on the ball a laurel wreath within which is the Sphinx resting on a tablet inscribed "Egypt"; below, a scroll inscribed "The Lancashire Fusiliers". For officers the grenade and detail on the ball are in gilt or gilding metal; the title scroll is in silver plate. For other ranks the badge is in gilding metal.

THE GRENADE is common to all Fusilier regiments who have a distinguishing device on the ball, in this case a laurel wreath with the Sphinx and "Egypt" within it.

The badge of the Sphinx with "Egypt" was granted to the 20th Foot by Horse Guards Letter No. 170 of 6th July, 1802, for service against the French in 1801. (See Appendix 3.)

The regiment was raised in 1688, being numbered the 20th Foot in 1751, to which "East Devonshire" was added in 1782. On the reorganization of the infantry in 1881 it obtained its present title, hence "The Lancashire Fusiliers" on the scroll below the badge.

This is one of the six "Minden" regiments, and unconfirmed statements assert that the laurel wreath is in memory of the battle on 1st August, 1759.

A grenade with the Royal Arms on the ball. The officers'
badge is made in gilt and that for other ranks in gilding
metal. As in all Fusilier regiments, the badge is a grenade,
the distinguishing device on the ball being the Royal Arms.
The flames in the officers' badges are elongated and taller
than those depicted.

THIS REGIMENT was raised in 1678 and is described as "Fusiliers"
in 1691; it was probably Fusiliers earlier.

In the Royal Warrant of 1st July, 1751, it was authorized to
bear on its Colours certain Royal Badges—viz., in the centre
the Thistle within the circle of St. Andrew, with the Crown
over it, and in the three corners of the second Colour the King's
Cypher and Crown above.

On the clothing badge these royal items are expressed in the
Royal Arms on the ball of the grenade.

On an eight-pointed star a circle inscribed "The Cheshire Regiment", within the circle an Acorn, in a vertical position, between Oak-leaves; on the inside of the outer rim of the circle is a rope motif. For officers the star is in silver plate, and the remainder gilt, the acorn on a background of green enamel. For other ranks the badge is in gilding metal.

THE STAR resembles the Star of the Order of the Garter. No satisfactory evidence has been produced regarding the origin of the Acorn and Oak-leaves. It has been stated that these were granted by George II for service at the battle of Dettingen on 27th June, 1743, but there is no evidence that any member of the regiment was at that battle. Neither does it bear the battle honour for that action.

The regiment was raised in 1689, being numbered 22nd Foot in 1751, to which "Cheshire" was added in 1782. When numbers were dropped from regimental designations in 1881 the title became "The Cheshire Regiment" as inscribed on the badge.

A grenade, on the ball of which is a circle inscribed "Royal Welch Fusiliers"; within the circle the Prince of Wales's plume with coronet and motto "Ich Dien" (I Serve). The badge is in bronze for officers and gilding metal for other ranks. The grenade is common to all Fusilier regiments, the distinguishing device on the ball of this regiment being the inscribed regimental title and Prince of Wales's plume. The flames of the grenade are somewhat unusual in design, being in two tiers.

THE REGIMENT was raised in 1689, and in the Royal Warrant of 23rd April, 1713, dealing with precedence of regiments it is described as "The Royal Regiment of Welsh Fusiliers." The present form (and spelling of "Welch") was adopted in 1920 (Army Order 56 of 1920), hence "Royal Welch Fusiliers" inscribed on the circle.

Under the Royal Warrant of 1st July, 1751, the regiment was authorized to bear in the centre of its Colours "the device of the Prince of Wales, viz. three Feathers issuing out of the Prince's Coronet."

*Within an unbroken wreath of immortelles, a Sphinx
resting on a tablet inscribed "Egypt"; on the lower portion
of the wreath the burnished letters "SWB". The badge
is in silver plate for officers and for other ranks the wreath
is in gilding metal and remainder in white metal.*

IMMORTELLES ARE plants of the "everlasting" class—*i.e.*, their
flowers do not lose their colour when they are dried. The deeds
for which this regiment was granted a wreath are certainly in the
category that shall never be forgotten. On 22nd January, 1879,
during the Zulu War, most of the companies of the 1st Battalion
24th Foot (as this regiment was at that time) were at Isandhlwana,
having the Queen's Colour with them. Here they were overwhelmed by a great army of Zulus and slaughtered almost to a
man. When the Commanding Officer, Colonel Pulleine, saw
that it was evident all would be lost, he ordered Lieutenant
Melvill to take the Colour and try to save it, by getting back to
the remaining companies at Helpmakaar, across the Buffalo River.
On his way to the river he was joined by Lieutenant Coghill,
who had been sent back owing to a severely injured knee. Both

young officers were mounted, but the track to the river was strewn with boulders, making progress slow and difficult—in fact, some swift Zulus came near enough to throw their spears at them. On reaching the river it was found to be in flood. Melvill stripped the Colour from off its pike and both officers plunged into the torrent. Coghill reached the other side safely, but on looking back saw Melvill in difficulties; he had become separated from his horse and had been washed against a rock in midstream, with the Zulus firing at him. Coghill at once rode back into the river, but his horse was instantly killed. Melvill could not hold on to the Colour, which the swift current tore from his grasp. Both officers reached the far bank safely, but in a very exhausted condition, and were soon done to death by some Zulus who had crossed lower down.

Elated by their great success at Isandhlwana, the Zulu army raced on to Rorkes Drift, where there was only one company of the 2nd Battalion 24th Foot, under Lieutenant G. Bromhead. with some personnel of the Royal Engineers and other corps, about 100 all ranks, under the command of Lieutenant J. M. Chard, R.E. When Chard and Bromhead learned of the disaster at Isandhlwana they immediately took measures to protect their small post. In the afternoon of 22nd January, about 600 Zulus approached the post, soon followed by the main body, estimated at 3,000. The little garrison, firing with great accuracy, kept the enemy at bay for a time, but were gradually pressed back. The Zulus set the hospital on fire and by its light the British were able to pick off the enemy better. When dawn came on the 23rd, no Zulus were seen except for over 350 dead that lay in front of the post, the remainder having retired.

The news of this heroic stand by a handful of British soldiers against enormous odds thrilled all Britain and did something to assuage the anguish of Isandhlwana.

The bodies of Melvill and Coghill were found by a search party on 4th February, 1879, and also the Colour case and crest at the head of the pike. Eventually the Colour itself was lifted from the water where it had become wedged between some boulders.

As soon as the regiment came home in the summer of 1880, Queen Victoria expressed a wish to see the Colour, and it was taken to Osborne House, Isle of Wight, for her inspection, to the pike of which Her Majesty attached a wreath of immortelles. Later the Queen commanded that "As a lasting token of her act in placing a wreath on the Queen's Colour, 1st Battalion 24th Regiment, to commemorate the devotion displayed by Lieutenants Melvill and Coghill, in their heroic endeavour to save the Colour on 22nd January, 1879, and of the noble defence of Rorkes Drift, Her Majesty has been graciously pleased to command that a silver wreath shall in future be borne round the staff of the Queen's Colour of the 24th Regiment."

These silver wreaths were borne by both battalions of The South Wales Borderers, and the original wreath with which the Queen decorated the Colour of the 1st Battalion is preserved in the Officers' Mess.

For the grant of the Sphinx superscribed "Egypt" see Appendix 3. "SWB" are the initial letters of The South Wales Borderers.

THE KING'S OWN SCOTTISH BORDERERS

Within a circle inscribed "King's Own Scottish Borderers" the Castle of Edinburgh with flags flying to the left from the top of each tower; above the circle, a scroll inscribed with the motto "In Veritate Religionis Confido" (In True Religion is My Trust), and below the circle a scroll inscribed with the motto "Nisi Dominus Frustra" (Unless the Lord be with me all is in vain); outside the circle a wreath of thistles; the Royal Crest above the first motto; St. Andrew's Cross overall and intertwined with the circle and motto scrolls. For officers the badge is in silver; the cross burnished, and white metal for other ranks.

THE REGIMENT was raised at Edinburgh on 19th March, 1689, hence the Castle of Edinburgh and the city's two mottoes in the badge. The Thistle and St. Andrew's Cross are Scottish emblems and therefore appropriate for this regiment. The Castle, Royal Crest and mottoes are mentioned in Queen's Regulations of

1844 to be borne on Colours; they were probably authorized earlier.

The regiment was numbered 25th Foot in 1751, "Sussex" being added in 1782. In 1805 the title became "The King's Own Borderers," and in 1870 "The York Regiment (King's Own Borderers)." It was not until 1881 that it became "The King's Own Scottish Borderers," as inscribed on the circle.

A mullet (five-pointed star) above a bugle stringed; issuing from each end of the bugle and enclosing the mullet, a spray of thistles. The mullet has one point uppermost. For officers the badge is in silver plate, and white metal for other ranks.

THE REGIMENT was raised in April, 1689, under the colonelcy of the young Earl of Angus. The mullet is from his coat of arms as a member of the Douglas family (Dukes of Hamilton). The bugle is common to all Rifle and Light Infantry regiments (see Appendix 5). Being a Scottish regiment, the thistles are appropriate as an embellishment to the badge.

The 2nd Battalion was raised in 1794 as The 90th Perthshire Volunteers by Mr. Thomas Graham, later Lord Lynedoch; it became a Light Infantry Corps in 1815, hence the bugle in its badge.

A Grenade, on the ball of which is the Castle of Inniskilling with St. George's flag flying to the right from the central tower; below the castle, the word "Inniskilling" on a scroll. The grenade is in gilt and the castle and scroll are in silver plate for officers; for other ranks the corresponding metals are gilding metal and white metal.

THE REGIMENT was formed in 1689 by William III from the defenders of Enniskillen when it was besieged by the forces of King James; hence the Castle of Inniskilling and name on the scroll on the ball of the grenade, the grenade being common to all Fusilier regiments.

In 1881 the old 27th Foot was linked with the 108th (Madras Infantry) Regiment and the Fermanagh, Royal Tyrone, Londonderry and Donegal Militias, from which time it assumed its present title. "Inniskilling" in the title and on the ball of the grenade is the former spelling of "Enniskillen." H.R.H. The Duke of Gloucester, Earl of Ulster, is Colonel-in-Chief of the regiment.

The Sphinx resting on a pedestal inscribed "Egypt" within two sprigs of laurel; below the laurel, a scroll inscribed "Gloucestershire". For officers the badge is in gold embroidery (originally silver), and white metal for other ranks. See Appendix 3 for a brief account of the service for which this badge was granted.

IN 1881 the 28th (North Gloucestershire) Regiment was amalgamated with the 61st (South Gloucestershire) Regiment to form the present regiment; hence "Gloucestershire" in the badge.

To The Gloucestershire Regiment belongs the unique distinction of wearing the Sphinx badge at the back of their headdress as well as in the front (or at the left side) in commemoration of the old 28th fighting back-to-back in the action on 21st March, 1801. This honour was confirmed to the regiment in 1830 by Horse Guards letter dated 11th May, 1830, which runs as follows:

Sir,

Referring to your letter of the 6th inst., I have the honour to acquaint you that it was never the intention to deprive the 28th Regiment of any badge of honour they may have acquired by their distinguished service in Egypt, and that there will be no objection to their retaining the plate they have been accustomed to *wear on the back of their caps* since that service, for which this letter may be shown by you to the Inspecting General Officer as sufficient authority.

I have, etc.,

(*Signed*) H. TAYLOR (A.G.)

To Lieut.-Colonel Haile,
Commanding 28th Regiment,
Buttevant.

An eight-pointed elongated star of 48 rays, thereon an oval Garter; within the Garter the lion of the Royal Crest upon a tablet inscribed "FIRM". The star is in silver plate and the Garter in gilt or gilding metal for officers and white metal and gilding metal for other ranks.

THE 1ST BATTALION of this regiment, the old 29th Foot, was raised by Colonel Thomas Farrington of the Coldstream Guards in 1694, and a number of later Colonels also came from the Coldstream Guards. For this reason the general outline of the star is similar to that of the Coldstream Guards, which is the Star of the Order of the Garter, and the Garter in the badge of The Worcestershire Regiment is derived from that connection also. The Lion of the Royal Crest was borne by the 29th towards the end of the eighteenth century, and the motto "FIRM" was borne by the 2nd Battalion, the old 36th Foot, in the early part of the nineteenth century.

A unique feature of the design of the Garter is the end of the buckle. This resembles three pears, which are traditionally considered to allude to the three black pears in the Arms of the City of Worcester.

This regiment also wears a star on the valise carried on the back. It was officially confirmed to the regiment "as a special distinction for service in the field" by Horse Guards letter of 7th August, 1877.

THE EAST LANCASHIRE REGIMENT

The Sphinx resting on a tablet inscribed "Egypt", below the tablet a rose, the whole within a laurel wreath; a crown surmounts the wreath; resting on the lower portion of the wreath, a scroll inscribed "East Lancashire". The badge is in silver plate, except the Rose, which is gilt for officers and gilding metal for other ranks.

THE 1ST BATTALION was the old 30th Foot and was awarded the Sphinx over "Egypt" for service against the French in 1801 (see Appendix 3). The rose is the Red Rose of Lancaster.

In 1782 "Cambridgeshire" was added to 30th Foot as the title of the 1st Battalion. The 2nd Battalion was the old 59th Foot, and had "2nd Nottinghamshire" added to its number in 1782. When these two regiments were amalgamated in 1881 the first title was The West Lancashire Regiment, which a few weeks later was altered to "East Lancashire" as inscribed on the scroll.

THE EAST SURREY REGIMENT

An eight-pointed star, the top point displaced by a crown which rests upon a shield bearing the Arms of Guildford (viz. the Castle of Guildford, with a lion couchant guardant on a mount in front of the castle and a woolpack on either side); superimposed on the central turret is the Arms of Kingston-upon-Thames—below, a scroll inscribed "East Surrey". The badge is in bronze for officers, and for other ranks the star and castle are in white metal and the crown, scroll and shield are in gilding metal.

THE 1ST BATTALION was raised in 1702, numbered 31st Foot in 1751 to which "Huntingdonshire" was added in 1782. The 2nd Battalion was raised as a 2nd Battalion to the 31st in 1756, became a separate regiment two years later and designated "70th Foot (Glasgow Greys)," having been raised in and about Glasgow: in 1782 it became "70th (or The Surrey) Regiment," and in 1813 "Glasgow Lowland" displaced "The Surrey." These two regiments, 31st and 70th, were amalgamated in 1881 to form The East Surrey Regiment; hence the inscription on the scroll and the Arms of Guildford, Surrey's county town, on the star.

THE DUKE OF CORNWALL'S
LIGHT INFANTRY

A bugle with strings; resting on each end of the bugle, a scroll inscribed "Cornwall"; above the scroll, a coronet. The strings pass upwards from the bugle, behind the scroll to the centre of the base of the coronet. The badge is in silver plate for officers and white metal for other ranks. The badge is backed by a piece of semi-circular red cloth which does not project beyond any portion of the badge.

THE IST BATTALION was designated "32nd (Cornwall) Regiment" in 1782, but in recognition of its gallant services in the defence of the Residency at Lucknow during the Indian Mutiny it was honoured by being made a Light Infantry Corps. On being amalgamated with the 46th (South Devonshire) Regiment in 1881 the title of the new regiment became The Duke of Cornwall's Light Infantry; hence the bugle in the badge and the word "Cornwall." The coronet is that of the Prince of Wales, as in the Great Seal of the Duke of Cornwall.

The red cloth backing commemorates service in a Light Infantry Battalion in 1777 at Brandywine during the War of American Independence.

THE DUKE OF WELLINGTON'S
REGIMENT (WEST RIDING)

*The crest and motto of the Duke of Wellington, above a
scroll inscribed "The West Riding". The heraldic description of the crest is: Out of a ducal coronet, or, a demi-lion
rampart, gu., holding a forked pennon, of the last, flowing
to the sinister, one-third per pale from the staff, arg.,
charged with the Cross of St. George. The motto is
"Virtutis Fortuna Comes" (Fortune favours the Brave).
The badge is in silver plate for officers, except the title
scroll which is in gilt or gilding metal, and in white metal
and gilding metal for other ranks.*

THE GREAT Duke of Wellington had a long association with this
regiment. He was a Subaltern in the 76th Foot (later 2nd Battalion) in 1787, and a Major in the 33rd (later 1st Battalion) in
1793, and Colonel of the 33rd from 1806 to 1816.

In 1782 the 33rd had added to its number "1st Yorkshire,
West Riding," but when the Duke of Wellington died in 1852

the Queen granted the regiment as its secondary title "The Duke of Wellington's" in honour of the great Duke (*London Gazette*, 28th June, 1853).

When the 33rd and 76th were amalgamated in 1881 the title became "The Halifax Regiment (Duke of Wellington's)," which changed a few weeks later to "The Duke of Wellington's (West Riding Regiment)"; hence "The West Riding" on the scroll.

The present form of the title was adopted in 1920.

THE BORDER REGIMENT

A star similar to that of the Order of the Garter, but with a crown displacing the uppermost point; on the star another star similar to that of the Order of the Bath, on the four arms of which are inscribed battle honours; in the centre of the latter star a circle inscribed "Arroyo dos Molinos 1811", and within the circle a Dragon superscribed "China" on a ground of one-third white (above) and two-thirds red (below); below the latter star, a laurel wreath; on the bottom portion of the former star, a scroll inscribed "The Border Regt." The badge is in silver plate for officers and white metal for other ranks.

THE REGIMENT was formed in 1881 by amalgamating the 34th Cumberland Regiment with the 55th Westmorland Regiment under the title "The Border Regiment" as on the scroll.

The old Westmorland Militia had a garter star in their badge, which might have suggested the first star in this badge. "Arroyo dos Molinos 1811" refers to an action in the Peninsular War which occurred on 28th October, 1811: the 34th Foot captured its opposite number in the French Army, together with its band and drums, and The Border Regiment is the only regiment to bear the battle honour "Arroyo dos Molinos." (In passing, it may be noted that there is no such place as Arroyo dos Molinos: the correct name is Arroyo Molinos, meaning "stream of the mill": Arroyo dos Molinos means "two mill streams." See Fortescue's *History of the British Army*, Vol. VIII, p. 272.) The China Dragon superscribed "China" was granted to the 55th for service during the China War of 1840–42. The laurel wreath is believed to have been granted for service at Fontenoy in 1745.

THE ROYAL SUSSEX REGIMENT

The Star of the Order of the Garter over the Roussillon plume, with a scroll below inscribed "The Royal Sussex Regiment". For officers the star is in silver plate, the Cross of St. George in red enamel on a silver-plate ground, and the Garter and motto are on a blue ground. The plume is in silver plate except for the stem, which is gilt. For other ranks the badge is in white metal with scroll in gilding metal.

THE SUSSEX MILITIA had the Star of the Order of the Garter as their badge, possibly because the Duke of Richmond, whilst Colonel of the Regiment, had the Order conferred upon him. The Regular regiment seems to have adopted this star. The 1st Battalion, the old 35th Foot, fought under Wolfe at Quebec on 13th September, 1759, at which victory they were opposed to the French Regiment of Royal Roussillon, whom they defeated, taking from their hats the long white plumes and sticking them in their own. The Roussillon plume was granted to The Royal Sussex Regiment as a badge in 1901.

In 1782 the 35th had "Dorsetshire" added to its designation, this being changed to "Sussex" in 1805; it was granted "Royal" under *London Gazette* of 15th June, 1832. In 1881 the 35th was linked with the 107th (Bengal Infantry) to form the present regiment.

THE ROYAL HAMPSHIRE REGIMENT

OFFICERS   OTHER RANKS

Officers: An eight-pointed silver-plated star, on the centre of which the Garter with motto on a ground of blue enamel, surmounted by a crown in gilt which displaces the uppermost point of the star. Within the Garter the Hampshire Rose in gilt and red enamel. On the lower part of the star a scroll inscribed "Royal Hampshire" on a ground of blue enamel. Other ranks: The Hampshire Rose with, above, the Royal Tiger standing on a scroll, the whole enclosed in a laurel wreath on the lower part of which is a scroll inscribed "Royal Hampshire", the tiger, crown and wreath in white metal and rose and scroll in gilding metal. (This is identical with the former badge except for the addition of "Royal" to the scroll and the crown above the tiger.)

UP TO April, 1949, the badge was the Hampshire Rose with the Royal Tiger standing on a scroll above, the whole enclosed in a laurel wreath; on the lower part of the wreath a scroll inscribed "Hampshire."

The Hampshire Rose is a red rose, a badge of Henry V, who, according to tradition, conferred it upon the city of Winchester in 1415 as he passed through on his way to Agincourt. It is incorporated into the Arms of the county.

The Royal Tiger was granted to the regiment in commemoration of the services of the 67th Foot (later 2nd Battalion) in India from 1805 to 1826.

In recognition of its past services the regiment was granted the title "Royal" in November, 1946, thus becoming The Royal Hampshire Regiment. In consequence of this the cap badges were re-designed and announced in April, 1949.

THE SOUTH STAFFORDSHIRE REGIMENT

The Stafford Knot surmounted by a crown; below the knot, a scroll inscribed "South Staffordshire". The knot and crown are in silver plate and the scroll in gilt or gilding metal for officers and in white metal and gilding metal for other ranks.

THE KNOT was a badge of the De Stafford family and has been incorporated into the Arms of Staffordshire and Stafford.

The 1st Battalion of the regiment was designated "38th (1st Staffordshire) Regiment" in 1782; the 2nd Battalion, the old 80th, had "Staffordshire Volunteers" as its secondary title in 1795. In 1881 the 38th and 80th were linked to form the present regiment; hence "South Staffordshire" on the scroll. As one of the County regiments the knot is appropriate as its badge, which was also worn by the County Militia.

Behind their badges the regiment are authorized to wear a piece of brown holland material to commemorate a period of about sixty years' service (1706-1762) in the West Indies during which, being neglected by the home authorities, they mended their clothing with holland material instead of cloth.

The Castle of Gibraltar with a key depending from the centre of the base; above the castle, the Sphinx resting on a tablet inscribed "Marabout"; below the castle, a scroll inscribed with the motto "Primus in Indis" (First in India); a laurel wreath encloses the castle and motto, and this is continued below the castle by a scroll inscribed "Dorsetshire". The castle, motto, Sphinx and "Marabout" are in silver plate and the remainder gilt for officers and gilding metal for other ranks.

FOR THE award of the castle and key for service at Gibraltar see Appendix 2, and for the Sphinx see Appendix 3. Fort Marabout was held by the French during the Egyptian Campaign of 1801, and was captured by the 54th Regiment, later the 2nd Battalion of the regiment.

"Primus in Indis" was granted to the 39th Regiment in recognition of its being the first crown regiment to serve in active operations in India; it served under Robert Clive at the Battle of Plassey, which took place on 23rd June, 1757, for which it bears the battle honour "Plassey" on its Colours.

In 1782 the 39th had "East Middlesex" added to its number, but this was changed to "Dorsetshire" in 1807. The 2nd Battalion, the old 54th, had "West Norfolk" added to its number in 1782. When these two regiments were amalgamated in 1881 the title became The Dorsetshire Regiment; hence the name on the scroll below the castle.

THE SOUTH LANCASHIRE REGIMENT
(THE PRINCE OF WALES'S
VOLUNTEERS)

*The Prince of Wales's plume, coronet and motto "Ich Dien" (I serve); below, the Sphinx resting on a tablet inscribed "Egypt"; above the Prince of Wales's plume, a scroll inscribed "South Lancashire" and below the Sphinx and tablet, a scroll inscribed "Prince of Wales's Vols.";
branches of laurel connect the ends of the scrolls. The centre features, except coronet, are in silver plate, remainder in gilt for officers and in white metal and gilding metal for other ranks.*

THE 2ND BATTALION, the old 82nd Foot, was designated "Prince of Wales's Volunteers" when it was raised in 1793; hence the Prince of Wales's plume, coronet and motto in the badge. The Sphinx was granted to the 1st Battalion, the old 40th Foot (see Appendix 3).

Before 1881 the 1st Battalion was designated the "40th (or 2nd Somersetshire) Regiment" and the 2nd Battalion the "82nd

(Prince of Wales's Volunteers)," but when they were linked in that year the resultant title was "The South Lancashire Regiment (Prince of Wales's Volunteers)," only to be altered a few weeks later to "The Prince of Wales's Volunteers (South Lancashire Regiment)." A reversion to the first arrangement of the title, as it stands today, was sanctioned in 1938 (Army Order 244/1938). The inscriptions on the scrolls are merely portions of the title.

THE WELCH REGIMENT

The Prince of Wales's plume, coronet and motto; below, a scroll inscribed "The Welch". For officers the badge is in bronze; for other ranks the feathers and motto ("Ich Dien"—I serve) are in white metal and the remainder in gilding metal.

THE 1ST BATTALION, the old 41st Foot, was raised in 1719 as an Invalid Corps, and became a Foot Regiment in 1787; "The Welsh" was added to its number in 1831. In 1881 it was amalgamated with the 69th, South Lincolnshire Regiment, under the title "The Welsh Regiment." The revised spelling of "Welch" was adopted in 1920, hence "The Welch" on the scroll.

Being a regiment of the Principality, the Prince of Wales's plume is most appropriate as a badge.

THE BLACK WATCH
(ROYAL HIGHLAND REGIMENT)

For officers the Star of the Order of the Thistle, diamond cut, in silver plate; on the Star a thistle wreath in gilt or gilding metal; within the wreath an oval inscribed "Nemo me impune lacesset" in gilt or gilding metal; above the oval, a crown in gilt or gilding metal; within the oval on a recessed seeded ground, St. Andrew with cross in silver plate; below the wreath, the Sphinx in gilt or gilding metal; above the oval scrolls inscribed "The Royal Highlanders", and below the oval scrolls inscribed "Black Watch". For other ranks, the whole in white metal.

AS THE senior Highland regiment, the Star of the Order of the Thistle is appropriate to this old corps, raised in 1739. As the 42nd Royal Highland Regiment it fought in the Egyptian Campaign of 1801, where it gained the Sphinx badge.

The regiment was raised to suppress lawlessness among the disaffected Highlanders, following the failure of the 1715 Rebellion in support of the Old Pretender. Soon after it became known, as a kind of nickname, as the Black Watch, in Gaelic "Am Freiceadan Dubh." There are two possible origins of the term: it may have been used by the disaffected as a term of contempt for their own countrymen to distinguish them from the English soldiers or "Watchers," whom they referred to as "Saighdearn Dearg" (Red Soldiers); or it may have been suggested by the sombre colour of the tartan adopted by the regiment.

"Black Watch" was not officially incorporated into the regimental designation until July, 1861.

The regiment at present wears no badge in its headdress but carries a red hackle in its place.

THE OXFORDSHIRE AND
BUCKINGHAMSHIRE LIGHT INFANTRY

*A bugle horn with strings, the strings tied in three loops.
The badge is in silver plate for officers and white metal for
other ranks.*

THIS REGIMENT was formed in 1881 by amalgamating the 43rd
Monmouthshire Light Infantry with the 52nd Oxfordshire Light
Infantry under the title "The Oxfordshire Light Infantry."
"Buckinghamshire" was added in 1908.

Both the 43rd and 52nd were converted to Light Infantry in
1803 and gained a great reputation in the Light Division during
the Peninsular War. See Appendix 5 regarding bugle badges.

Major-General Sir John Moore, of Corunna fame, was Colonel
of the 52nd in the early part of the nineteenth century. He was
the "father" of Light Infantry and his regiment was the first to
be converted to that role, the 43rd being converted a few months
later.

The Castle of Gibraltar with a key depending from the centre of the base; above the castle, the Sphinx on a tablet inscribed "Egypt"; the whole, with the exception of the Sphinx, enclosed in an oak wreath; on the lower portion of the wreath, a scroll inscribed "The Essex Regt." In silver plate for officers, and for other ranks the castle and wreath are in gilding metal and Sphinx and Scroll in white metal.

THE CASTLE and key of Gibraltar was granted to the 56th Foot (later 2nd Battalion) for service at the siege in 1779-83 (see Appendix 2). The Sphinx with "Egypt" was granted to the 44th Foot (later 1st Battalion) for service in the Egyptian Campaign of 1801. (See Appendix 3.)

The 44th, East Essex Regiment and the 56th, West Essex Regiment were amalgamated in 1881 under the designation "The Essex Regiment"; hence the inscription on the scroll.

The Essex Militia had an oak wreath in their badge, traditionally associated with King Charles hiding in the oak tree.

THE SHERWOOD FORESTERS (NOTTINGHAMSHIRE AND DERBYSHIRE REGIMENT)

A Maltese Cross surmounted by a crown; in the centre a wreath of oak, within the wreath a stag lodged; on the left arm of the cross and across the left branch of the wreath, a straight scroll inscribed "Sherwood"; on the right arm of the cross and across the right branch of the wreath, a straight scroll inscribed "Foresters"; below the cross, a scroll inscribed "Notts & Derby". In bronze for officers; for other ranks it is in white metal, with the exception of the scroll, which is in gilding metal.

THE MALTESE CROSS, oak wreath and stag are derived from the badge of the old 95th (Derbyshire) Regiment which was linked with the 45th (1st Nottinghamshire) Regiment in 1881 to form the present regiment. The regiment's home is in the Sherwood Forest country, hence the regiment's main title and inscription on the straight scrolls of the badge.

The old Nottinghamshire Militia had an oak wreath in their badge in allusion to Sherwood Forest, and this may have suggested the wreath in the Regular regiment's badge.

Two Royal stags form the supporters to the Arms of the city of Nottingham.

THE LOYAL REGIMENT
(NORTH LANCASHIRE)

The Royal Crest (i.e., Lion upon the crown); below the crown a rose; below the rose a scroll inscribed "The Loyal Regiment". For officers, the rose in gilt with red enamel petals and green points, the Royal Crest above in silver plate and the scroll below in gilt or gilding metal. For other ranks, the Royal Crest is in white metal and the rose and scroll in gilding metal.

THE 47TH FOOT, which became the 1st Battalion of the regiment in 1881, had "The Lancashire" added to its number in 1782, and eventually adopted the crest of the Duchy of Lancaster—*i.e.*, the Royal Crest—as a badge. The rose in the badge is the Red Rose of Lancaster.

The 81st Foot, which became the 2nd Battalion in 1881, had as its secondary title in 1832 "Loyal Lincoln Volunteers" (*London Gazette* of 20th April, 1832), having been raised in Lincolnshire in 1793 by Colonel Albemarle Bertie, later ninth Earl of Lindsey, whose motto is "Loyaute m'oblige" (My loyalty compels me).

The 47th and 81st were amalgamated in 1881 under the title "The Loyal North Lancashire Regiment," the present arrangement for the title being adopted in 1920; hence the inscription on the scroll.

In 1934 the regiment adopted "Loyaute m'oblige" as its motto.

The Castle and Key of Gibraltar within a laurel wreath; above the castle a scroll inscribed "Gibraltar", and below the castle a scroll inscribed "Talavera". On the lower part of the stems of the wreath a scroll inscribed "Northamptonshire". For officers the whole of the badge is in silver, with the exception of the scroll inscribed "Northamptonshire", which is made of gilt or gilding metal. For other ranks the corresponding portions are in white metal and gilding metal.

THE BADGE of the Castle and Key superscribed "Gibraltar, 1779–83," with the motto "Montis Insignia Calpe," was granted to the 58th Foot (now 2nd Bn. The Northamptonshire Regiment) for bearing on Regimental Colours, by *London Gazette* notice of 13th May, 1836, to commemorate the service of that regiment in the defence of Gibraltar. Most of the features of this badge were incorporated into the badge on the Glengarry cap of the 58th in 1871.

A brief account of this siege of Gibraltar is at Appendix 2.

The word "Talavera" as a battle honour was granted to the 48th by *London Gazette* notice of 12th November, 1816, in commemoration of the distinguished services by both the 1st and 2nd Battalions, 48th Foot, at the Battle of Talavera on 27th-28th July, 1809, during the Peninsular War.

During the action the 1st/48th was in Stewart's brigade and the 2nd/48th in Tilson's, both brigades being in the 2nd Division, commanded by Major-General Hill, which held the key to Sir Arthur Wellesley's position, the Cerro De Medellin, a hill on the left of his line. Before the Division could take up its position the French occupied the hill during darkness on 27th July, but a charge by the 1st/48th and 29th drove them off with heavy loss.

On 28th July, Marshal Victor, the French Commander, massed his attack against Wellesley's left flank with the intention of capturing the Cerro De Medellin.

They attacked with great fury, but were halted by the accurate fire of the 2nd Division, which then charged and drove the enemy headlong back. During the afternoon the Guards and the King's German Legion pressed a counter-attack too far and got into difficulties with the French second line. When Wellesley noticed their plight he called to one of his staff, "Where is the 48th? Send the 48th to bring them out." The 48th came down the Cerro De Medellin at full speed and, after letting the retreating crowds pass through their ranks, "resumed its proud and beautiful line, marched against the right of the pursuing columns, and plied with such destructive musketry, and closed upon them with such a firm and regular pace, that the forward movement of the French was checked" (Napier). Thus the 48th saved the day, and Wellesley suitably commended the regiment in his despatch on the battle.

The word "Talavera" was incorporated into the regimental badge in 1881, when the old 48th (Northamptonshire) Regiment was linked with the old 58th (Rutlandshire) Regiment to form the present regiment. Hence also the word "Northamptonshire" in the badge.

THE ROYAL BERKSHIRE REGIMENT
(PRINCESS CHARLOTTE OF WALES'S)

OFFICERS

OTHER RANKS

For officers: On three coils of rope in bronze, the China Dragon with crown above in silver plate, red enamel in the crown. For other ranks: The China Dragon above a scroll inscribed "Royal Berkshire". The badge is in gilding metal.

THE COILED cord in the officers' badges represents a coil of rope on board ship, in allusion to the fact that the 1st Battalion, the old 49th Foot, served as marines in Sir Hyde Parker's fleet at the battle of Copenhagen on 2nd April, 1801. The regiment was granted the battle honour "Copenhagen" in February, 1819. The Dragon was granted for service in the China War of 1840-42.

The 49th had "Hertfordshire" added to its designation in 1782, whilst the 66th, later 2nd Battalion, had "Berkshire" added at the same time. When the 49th and 66th were linked in 1881 the title became "Princess Charlotte of Wales's (Berkshire Regiment)." On 29th September, 1885, the regiment was granted the title "Royal" in recognition of the services of the 1st Battalion at the action at Tofrek, near Suakin on the Red Sea, on 22nd March, 1885 (General Order 107 of 1885). The present form of the title was adopted in 1920, hence "Royal Berkshire" on the scroll of the other ranks' badge.

On the beret a triangular red patch, 2 in. wide and $2\frac{1}{4}$ in. deep pointing downwards, is worn behind the badge of all ranks in recognition of the service of the Light Company of the 49th at Brandywine, in 1777, during the War of American Independence.

ROYAL MARINES

The Globe, showing the Eastern hemisphere, surmounted by the Royal Crest (Lion on crown) within a laurel wreath. For officers, the globe in silver and gilt, remainder in gilt. For marines, the badge is in gilding metal.

THIS BADGE was granted by King George IV in 1827 to symbolize the world-wide services of the Royal Marines. The laurel wreath was awarded as a distinction for service at the capture of the island of Belleisle, in the northern part of the Bay of Biscay, in 1761.

When the Royal Marines serve under the Army Act they take precedence next below The Royal Berkshire Regiment, the reason being that they were raised in 1755, *i.e.*, *after* the 49th, now The Royal Berkshire Regiment, whose date is 25th December, 1743, and *before* the 50th, now The Queen's Own Royal West Kent Regiment, raised December, 1755.

The Royal Marines are therefore placed here in their correct place in Army precedence.

THE QUEEN'S OWN
ROYAL WEST KENT REGIMENT

*The White Horse of Kent standing on a scroll inscribed
with the motto "Invicta" (Unconquered) in Old English
lettering; below the motto scroll another scroll inscribed
"Royal West Kent". The badge is in silver plate for
officers and white metal for other ranks.*

A WHITE HORSE rampant, with the motto "Invicta," was the Arms
of the ancient kingdom of Kent. The first invaders of Kent bore
a horse on their standards. This badge is therefore appropriate
to a Kent regiment. It was also borne by the old Kent Militia.

In 1782 the title of the 1st Battalion was "50th, or West Kent
Regiment," the latter portion being changed to "The Duke of
Clarence's" in 1827 and to "The Queen's Own" in 1831 on the
Duchess of Clarence becoming Queen Consort at the accession
of William IV. The 2nd Battalion was the 97th, Earl of Ulster's
Regiment. The 50th and 97th were amalgamated in 1881 under
the title "The Queen's Own Royal West Kent Regiment";
hence the inscription on the scroll.

THE KING'S OWN
YORKSHIRE LIGHT INFANTRY

A French horn with a rose in the twist. For officers the horn and the rose are in silver plate, the rose upon a black ground; for other ranks the whole in white metal.

THE FRENCH horn is a form of bugle. The 1st Battalion became a Light Infantry Corps in 1809 and designated 51st (2nd Yorkshire, West Riding) Light Infantry. The 2nd Battalion was raised by the Hon. East India Company in 1839 as the 2nd Madras European Regiment (Light Infantry), becoming the 105th Madras Light Infantry in 1861. On amalgamation in 1881 these two regiments, 51st and 105th, became the present regiment. See Appendix 5 for the adoption of the bugle by Light Infantry regiments. The rose in the badge is the White Rose of York, appropriate to a Yorkshire regiment.

The regiment had a close association with Major-General Sir John Moore, the "father" of Light Infantry, who was killed at the battle of Corunna on 16th January, 1809, in that he received his first commission into the 51st Foot.

THE KING'S SHROPSHIRE LIGHT INFANTRY

*A bugle horn stringed, the strings tied in three knots;
within the bend of the bugle and below the strings, on bars
the letters "KSLI". In silver with "KSLI" in gilt for
officers; the bugle is in white metal and the lettering is
gilding metal for other ranks.*

THE IST BATTALION, the old 53rd Foot, had "Shropshire" added
to its number in 1782. The 2nd Battalion was designated "85th
(Bucks Volunteers) Light Infantry" in 1808 and was granted
"King's" in 1821 (*London Gazette*, 21st April, 1821). When the
53rd and 85th were linked in 1881 the title became "The Shropshire Regiment (King's Light Infantry)," and a few weeks later
this was altered to "The King's Light Infantry (Shropshire Regiment)" and soon afterwards rearranged again to "The King's
(Shropshire Light Infantry)," but in 1920 the present form was
adopted, hence "KSLI".

See Appendix 5 for the bugle being the badge of all Light
Infantry regiments.

THE MIDDLESEX REGIMENT
(THE DUKE OF CAMBRIDGE'S OWN)

The Prince of Wales's plume, coronet and motto ("Ich Dien"—I serve); below, the coronet and cypher, "G", of H.R.H. The Duke of Cambridge; all within a laurel wreath; across the bottom of the wreath a scroll inscribed "Albuhera"; below the wreath a scroll inscribed "Middlesex Regiment". In silver plate for officers, and for other ranks the plume, motto and title scroll in white metal and remainder in gilding metal.

THIS REGIMENT was formed in 1881 by amalgamating the old "57th, West Middlesex Regiment" with the old "77th East Middlesex, or the Duke of Cambridge's Own Regiment," a title that was granted in 1876 (*London Gazette*, 20th June, 1876). The title of the amalgamated regiment was "The Middlesex Regiment (Duke of Cambridge's Own)." The Cypher of George, Duke of Cambridge, was "G", which is interlaced and reversed in the badge. The Prince of Wales's plume is an old badge of the 77th.

The battle of Albuhera was fought on 16th May, 1811, during the Peninsular War, when a small British force was nearly overwhelmed by a much stronger French force. Severe casualties reduced our regiments to mere skeletons, but they fought stubbornly and refused to give way. When Colonel Inglis, of the 57th, was wounded he would not allow himself to be carried from the field, but was placed near the Colours and shouted "Die hard, my men, die hard." This gave rise to the regiment's honoured nickname of "The Diehards" and explains why the battle honour "Albuhera" is inscribed on the badge.

For officers, a bugle with strings in silver plate on a scarlet cord boss. For other ranks, a Maltese Cross, on the top arm a tablet inscribed "Celer et Audax" (Swift and Bold); above the tablet a crown; in the centre of the cross a circle inscribed "The King's Royal Rifle Corps", within the circle a bugle with strings; battle honours are on each arm of the cross. The badge is in black metal with an edging of red cloth.

THE MALTESE CROSS is believed to have been derived from the badge of the old 5th Battalion. The motto "Celer et Audax" was granted for services in North America under Major-General James Wolfe in 1759 (*London Gazette*, 16th October, 1824).

The regiment was raised in 1755 as the 62nd Foot, but two years later became the 60th, Royal American Regiment. In 1824 its title was 60th, The Duke of York's Own Rifle Corps and Light Infantry; hence the bugle in the centre of the cross (see Appendix 5). In 1881 the title became "The King's Royal Rifle Corps" as inscribed on the circle.

THE WILTSHIRE REGIMENT
(DUKE OF EDINBURGH'S)

A cross pattee surmounted by the coronet of the late Duke of Edinburgh: in the centre on a convex plate the monogram "AEA" interlaced and reversed, surmounted by the coronet; below, a scroll inscribed "The Wiltshire Regiment". For officers the badge is in silver with a gilt centre plate. For other ranks, the whole in gilding metal.

BETWEEN 1874 and 1881 the Wiltshire Militia had a Maltese Cross in their badge, which might have suggested that in the badge of the Regular battalions.

The coronet and monogram "AEA" are those of the late Duke of Edinburgh, Alfred Ernest Albert, second son of Queen Victoria. In 1874 the 99th was granted the secondary title of "Duke of Edinburgh's": it became the 2nd Battalion of the regiment in 1881. The 1st Battalion was the former 62nd, which in 1782 had "Wiltshire" added to its designation.

In 1881 the 62nd and 99th were amalgamated under the title "The Wiltshire Regiment (Duke of Edinburgh's)"; hence the inscription on the scroll.

THE MANCHESTER REGIMENT

*A fleur-de-lis. In silver plate for officers and white metal
for other ranks.*

BEFORE 1923 the regimental badge was the Arms of the city of
Manchester, but in that year this was changed to the fleur-de-lis,
an old badge of the 63rd, which became the 1st Battalion on
linking with the 96th in 1881. In the second half of the eighteenth
and early part of the nineteenth century the 63rd had much
service against the French, which might account for its adoption
of the fleur-de-lis badge.

The 1st Battalion was raised in 1756 as the 2nd Bn. 8th Foot,
but two years later was constituted a separate corps and numbered
the 63rd. In 1782 "West Suffolk" was added to its numerical
designation. The 2nd Battalion was raised in 1824 and numbered
the 96th Foot. In 1881 the 63rd and 96th were amalgamated to
form one regiment designated The Manchester Regiment.

The Stafford Knot with the Prince of Wales's plume, coronet and motto "Ich Dien" (I serve) above; below the knot a scroll inscribed "North Stafford". For officers the knot and coronet are gilt or gilding metal, the plume and title scroll in silver plate; for other ranks the knot and coronet are in gilding metal and remainder in white metal.

THE KNOT was a badge of the De Stafford family and has been incorporated into the Arms of Staffordshire and Stafford. The 2nd Battalion, the former 98th Foot, was granted "Prince of Wales's" as a secondary title in 1876 (*London Gazette*, 27th October, 1876); hence the Prince of Wales's plume. The 1st Battalion was the old 64th, or 2nd Staffordshire Regiment, since 1782, but on the amalgamation of the two regiments in 1881 the title became "The Prince of Wales's (North Staffordshire Regiment)" but was altered to its present form in 1920; hence "North Stafford" on the scroll.

THE YORK AND LANCASTER
REGIMENT

*The Royal Tiger with the Union Rose above and a
coronet above the rose; the tiger is within a scroll inscribed
"York and Lancaster", with laurel continuing each arm of
the scroll upwards, meeting at the lower portion of the
coronet. Officers, tiger, wreath and scroll in gilt or
gilding metal, coronet in silver plate and rose in red and
white enamel and silver plate. Corresponding metals for
other ranks.*

BOTH BATTALIONS of this regiment served with distinction in
India during the early part of the nineteenth century as the 65th
and 84th Regiments respectively. By *London Gazette* notice of
12th April, 1823, the 65th was granted the badge of the Royal
Tiger in recognition of its Indian service. The 84th was granted
"York and Lancaster" as its secondary title in 1809, and probably
adopted the Union Rose as a badge soon afterwards. The ducal
coronet probably refers to the regiment's connection with the
Duchy of Lancaster. When the 65th and 84th were amalgamated
in 1881 the title became "The York and Lancaster Regiment."

A bugle with the strings taken upwards into a crown; within the strings the letters "DLI". The bugle is ornamented with a leaf motif. In silver plate for officers and white metal for other ranks.

THE 68TH FOOT had "Durham" added to its designation in 1782 and became a Light Infantry Corps in 1808. It became the 1st Battalion of the present regiment in 1881 on linking with the 106th Bombay Light Infantry, which had been a Light Infantry Corps from the time it was raised by the Hon. East India Company in 1839 as the 2nd Bombay European Regiment (Light Infantry); hence the bugle in the badge (see Appendix 5) On amalgamation in 1881 the title assumed was "The Durham Light Infantry," to which "DLI" in the badge refers.

THE HIGHLAND LIGHT INFANTRY
(CITY OF GLASGOW REGIMENT)

The Star of the Order of the Thistle, thereon a bugle horn; in the twist of the horn the monogram "HLI"; above the horn a crown, and below it an Elephant superscribed "Assaye" on a scroll. For officers the star and horn are in silver plate, the monogram, crown, elephant and "Assaye" are in gilt or gilding metal. The crown has a crimson cap. For other ranks the whole in white metal.

THE STAR of the Order of the Thistle is very appropriate to this Scottish regiment. The 71st, later 1st Battalion, was created a Light Infantry Corps in 1809, and on being linked with the 74th in 1881 the resultant title became "The Highland Light Infantry"; hence the bugle (see Appendix 5) and the monogram "HLI". "City of Glasgow Regiment" was added to the title under the authority of Army Order 221 of 1923. The Elephant superscribed "Assaye" was awarded to the 74th in recognition of its service under Sir Arthur Wellesley, later the great Duke of Wellington, at the battle of Assaye on 23rd September, 1803, against the Mahrattas.

THE SEAFORTH HIGHLANDERS
(ROSS-SHIRE BUFFS, THE DUKE OF ALBANY'S)

A Stag's head (no neck) above a scroll inscribed with the motto "Cuidich'n Righ" (Help the King). In silver plate for officers and white metal for other ranks. The officers' badge has the coronet and cypher "L" of H.R.H. the Duke of Albany between the antlers.

THE TRADITIONAL history of this badge, which is from the Arms of the Earl of Seaforth who raised the 72nd Foot, later 1st Battalion, in 1777, is that when in 1266 King Alexander II of Scotland was hunting in Mar Forest he was suddenly confronted by an infuriated stag, which charged him, knocked him off his horse and began to savage him on the ground. He shouted for help, and was promptly answered by Colin Fitzgerald, who rushed up and with a deft blow with his sword severed the animal's head immediately behind the antlers (hence no neck). In gratitude for saving his life the King granted Fitzgerald a stag's head with the motto "Cuidich'n Righ" as a badge to his coat of arms. One of Fitzgerald's descendants became the first Earl of Seaforth in 1623.

A Stag's head above a ducal coronet within a wreath of ivy; on the bottom of the wreath a scroll inscribed "Bydand" (translatable as "Stand Fast"). In silver plate for officers and white metal for other ranks.

THE GORDON HIGHLANDERS were formed in 1881 by amalgamating the old 75th Stirlingshire Regiment and the 92nd Gordon Highlanders under the new title of The Gordon Highlanders.

The 92nd was raised in 1794 by George, Marquess of Huntly, later Duke of Gordon, and the stag's head in a ducal coronet is the crest of the Gordon family.

When the 92nd was being raised Jean, Duchess of Gordon, took an active part in the recruiting of the regiment. She rode about the countryside to the fairs and "kissed" intending recruits by holding a shilling between her teeth, and the recruit had to take it with his teeth, the result being a "kiss." The bonnet that she wore is still a treasured possession of the regiment.

St. Andrew with Cross within a wreath of thistles; on the lower portion of the wreath a scroll inscribed "Cameron". In silver plate for officers and white metal for other ranks.

ST. ANDREW with Cross is from the badge of the Order of the Thistle, and therefore appropriate to this regiment, as also is the wreath of thistles which emphasizes its Scottish character. The word "Cameron" relates to Sir Alan Cameron, who raised the regiment in 1793.

Sir Alan Cameron was a remarkable man. As a young man he had to quit Scotland for having killed a kinsman in a duel caused by their mutual interest in a "fair widow." He went to Canada and joined the Royal Highland Emigrant Corps and fought in the American War of Independence. A few years later he married Miss Anne Philips, a Pembrokeshire heiress, who eloped with him to Gretna Green, where they were married.

*A harp surmounted by a crown, with a scroll below the
harp inscribed with the motto "Quis Separabit" (Who shall
separate us?). In silver plate for officers and white metal
for other ranks.*

THE HARP and crown are from the collar of the Order of
St. Patrick, and the motto is that of the Order, which was
instituted in 1783 by George III. (The bugle, which is common
to all Rifle regiments, is in the busby and shoulder belt badges.)

This regiment originated during the war against Revolutionary
France. The 83rd Foot (later 1st Battalion) and the 86th Foot
(later 2nd Battalion) were both raised in 1793. The 83rd was
raised in Dublin, and for many years "County of Dublin" was
part of its official title: the 86th was raised in Shropshire, Lancashire and the West Riding of Yorkshire and for a time "Leinster"
was in its title, but in 1812 this was changed to "Royal County
Down." In 1881 the 83rd and 86th were linked to form The
Royal Irish Rifles, they being the 1st and 2nd Battalions
respectively. In 1920 the title was altered to The Royal Ulster
Rifles, as at present.

THE ROYAL IRISH FUSILIERS
(PRINCESS VICTORIA'S)

This regiment wears two badges in its headdress, one above the other. The top badge is the coronet of Queen Victoria when Princess Victoria, and the bottom badge is a grenade, on the ball of which is the harp with the Prince of Wales's plume, coronet and motto "Ich Dien" (I serve) above. For officers the coronet, harp and Prince of Wales's plume, etc., are in silver, and the grenade is in gilt; for other ranks the corresponding metals are white metal and gilding metals.

THE CORONET is that of H.R.H. Princess Victoria, later Queen Victoria, and was adopted as a badge of the 89th Foot, later 2nd Battalion, to commemorate the presentation of Colours to the regiment by H.R.H. In 1866 "Princess Victoria's" was included in the regimental designation. The 87th, later 1st Battalion, were raised as the "Prince of Wales's Irish Regiment" in 1793 and were made "Fusiliers" in 1827 as the "87th or Royal Irish Fusiliers."

A circle inscribed "Argyll and Sutherland"; within the circle the cypher "L" of the late Princess Louise, interlaced and reversed; on the left of the cypher the Boar's head, and on the right the Cat; above the cypher and resting in the top part of the circle, the Princess's Coronet; the whole within a wreath of thistles. In silver for officers and white metal for other ranks.

THE 91ST FOOT, later 1st Battalion, had "Argyllshire" added to its number in 1820, and in 1872 "Princess Louise's" was added, the title then becoming "91st (Princess Louise's Argyllshire) Highlanders" (*London Gazette*, 2nd April, 1872). The 93rd, later 2nd Battalion, became the "Sutherland Highlanders" in 1861 (*London Gazette*, July, 1861). When the 91st and 93rd were amalgamated in 1881 the first title was "The Sutherland and Argyll Highlanders (Princess Louise's)."

As already mentioned, the cypher and coronet are those of the late Princess Louise. The Boar's head is the crest of the Argyll family and the Cat that of the Sutherland family.

THE RIFLE BRIGADE
(PRINCE CONSORT'S OWN)

A cross as in the Order of the Bath, thereon a circle inscribed "The Rifle Brigade" enclosing a bugle surmounted by a crown; the cross is enclosed within a wreath of laurel, which has twined around it a number of scrolls inscribed with battle honours; battle honours are also on each arm of the cross; above the top arm of the cross and connecting the upper ends of the wreath, a tablet inscribed "Waterloo" surmounted by a crown; on the lower portion of the wreath a scroll inscribed "Prince Consort's Own". In silver for officers and white metal for other ranks.

FORMED AS a Corps of Riflemen in 1800, it was numbered the 95th Foot in 1802. It served with distinction at the battle of Waterloo (18th June, 1815): in 1816 was taken out of the numbered regiments of the Line and designated "The Rifle Brigade" (*London Gazette*, 23rd February, 1816), and in 1862 "Prince Consort's Own" was added (*London Gazette*, 17th January, 1862), H.R.H. having been Colonel-in-Chief of the regiment from 23rd September, 1852, until his death on 14th December, 1861. The bugle is common to all Rifle regiments (see Appendix 5), and as these regiments do not carry Colours they place battle honours on their badges and appointments. The honour "Waterloo" was granted to the regiment by Horse Guards circular letter, 8th December, 1815.

ARMY AIR CORPS
THE GLIDER PILOT
AND PARACHUTE CORPS

*Members of the Glider Pilot Regiment originally wore the
Army Air Corps badge, which is an Eagle alighting upon
the uppermost of two bars carrying the letters "A.A.C"
within a laurel wreath and a crown above the Eagle. In
silver for officers and white metal for other ranks.*

THE EAGLE, the lord of the air, in the act of alighting represents
the operational mission of the regiment. The letters "A.A.C."
are the initials of the Corps.

The Army Air Corps was formed in February, 1942, under A.O.
21 of 1942 and comprised the Glider Pilot Regiment and Parachute Regiment. To these was added The Special Air Service
Regiment in April, 1944, which was disbanded in June, 1946,
but reconstituted in July, 1947.

The Parachute Regiment ceased to be a part of the A.A.C.
and became an Infantry Corps in August, 1949 (A.O. 97/1949).

In May, 1950, further changes took place under A.O. 66 of 1950, by which the A.A.C. was disbanded, The Glider Pilot and The Parachute Regiment were grouped together to form one Corps entitled "The Glider Pilot and Parachute Corps," and the Special Air Service Regiment was constituted a separate Corps.

Badges.—When the A.A.C. was in being the badge was as depicted above but was not worn by The Parachute Regiment, which had its own badge as depicted below.

The Glider Pilot Regiment now has its own badge as shown here, based on A.A.C. badge:

An Eagle alighting within scrolls inscribed "Glider Pilot Regiment," the eagle standing on the bottom scroll inscribed "Pilot"; the whole surmounted by a crown. Officers' badges in silver plate and other ranks' in white metal.

A pair of wings outspread horizontally straight, in the centre of which is an opened parachute surmounted by the Royal Crest (i.e., Lion on the crown). In silver for officers and white metal for other ranks.

THE WINGS and the parachute allude to the regiment's operational role.

21ST S.A.S. REGIMENT (ARTISTS) T.A.

The cap badge represents Mars and Minerva symbolizing the conjunction in the Artists Rifles of the Arts and War. Below is a scroll inscribed "Artists". The badge is in white metal. The Special Air Service Regiment cap badge also shown is worn by this unit as an arm badge. This badge symbolizes the role of the Special Air Service—a winged dagger striking downwards with the motto "Who dares wins". The embroidered badge is a white dagger with light blue wings piercing a light blue scroll, the whole edged with red, the wording in black; the whole on dark blue cloth.

THIS UNIT was raised in 1859, Lord Leighton, P.R.A., the eminent painter, being its first Colonel. In 1881 it was attached to The Rifle Brigade, but in 1908 was grouped with other London corps into The London Regiment, returning to The Rifle Brigade in 1937. Under Army Order 78 of 1947, it was transferred from "P" Corps of Infantry to the A.A.C. as the 21st Battalion, Special Air Service Regiment (Artists Rifles) (T.A.).

St. Andrew's Cross, thereon a thistle; below the thistle and twined round the lower portion of the cross, a scroll in two portions, the upper portion inscribed "Lowland" and the lower portion inscribed "Regiment". The badges were made in white metal.

THE LOWLAND REGIMENT was formed in January, 1942, and disbanded in December, 1949 (A.O. 150/1949).

A cross resembling St. Andrew's Cross, but sharpened at each point; on the cross a circular strap with the buckle on left side level with centre of the cross, on the opposite side a thistle; the circle inscribed at the top with "Highland" and on the bottom with "Regiment"; on the arms of the cross, and within the circle, two claymores, points uppermost; on the centre of the cross, a shield. The badges were made in white metal.

THE HIGHLAND REGIMENT was formed in January, 1943, and disbanded in December, 1949 (A.O. 150/1949).

Territorial Army Regiments and Units which have badges different from those of their Parent Regiment or Corps.

THE MONMOUTHSHIRE REGIMENT

1ST BATTALION   2ND BATTALION

The 1st Battalion was a Rifle unit, and its badge was the Welsh Dragon within a wreath composed of laurel, with Flanders poppies for the top portion; the wreath bears scrolls inscribed with battle honours, the whole ensigned with a crown. The 2nd Battalion's badge is the Welsh Dragon and the other ranks' badge is in gilding metal.

THE 1ST BATTALION originated in 1860 as the 1st Monmouthshire Rifle Volunteer Corps, but when it became affiliated to The South Wales Borderers the "1st" was omitted from its designation. In 1885 it became a Volunteer Battalion of The South Wales Borderers, but on the formation of the Territorial Force in 1908 it was re-designated as a battalion of The Monmouthshire Regiment, one of only four "regiments" of Infantry in the T.F.

The 2nd Battalion was also raised in 1860, when it was known as the 2nd Monmouthshire Rifle Volunteer Corps. Lady Hall, wife of Sir Benjamin Hall, later Lord Llanover, was responsible for the regimental motto "Gwell Angau Na Gwarth" (Rather death than dishonour) which she composed in 1864. She was an Englishwoman but was an enthusiast for the Volunteer Movement. In 1885 the title was altered to 2nd Volunteer Bn. The South Wales Borderers, becoming a battalion of The Monmouthshire Regiment in 1908.

BRECKNOCKSHIRE BATTALION
See THE MONMOUTHSHIRE REGIMENT

THE FIRST VOLUNTEER unit in Brecknockshire was raised in the 1860's, and at one time had a Mounted Infantry Company formed at Glosbury in 1884. On the formation of the Territorial Force in 1908, the county was the first to raise its allotted quota.

Its badge is the Red Dragon with the battle honour "South Africa, 1900-1901," a detachment having served with its parent regular regiment, The South Wales Borderers, in that campaign.

THE CAMBRIDGESHIRE REGIMENT

The badge is the Castle of Cambridge, on the central tower of which is a shield bearing the Arms of Ely; below, a scroll inscribed "The Cambridgeshire Regt."

A REGULAR REGIMENT designated "Cambridgeshire Regiment" was raised in 1702, at which time it was known as Colonel Saunderson's Regiment. In 1751 it was numbered the 30th Foot, and in 1782 "Cambridgeshire" was added. On the reorganization of the Infantry in 1881 the 30th was linked to the 59th to form The West Lancashire Regiment, which a few weeks later was altered to The East Lancashire Regiment, which title it still retains. Thus "Cambridgeshire" disappeared as a regular army title, but in 1860 the Cambridgeshire Rifle Volunteer Corps had been formed, which in 1887 became the 3rd (Cambridgeshire) Vol. Bn. The Suffolk Regiment. On the formation of the Territorial Force in 1908 its title became The Cambridgeshire Regiment, thus becoming one of the few "Regiments" of the Infantry of the Territorial Force. It is now 629 L.A.A. Regiment, R.A. (T.A.).

THE HERTFORDSHIRE REGIMENT

The badge is a hart lodged in water within a circle inscribed "The Hertfordshire Regiment", the whole surmounted by a crown.

IN 1794 the Hitchin Volunteers were formed, but were disbanded after the battle of Waterloo in 1815: on 25th October, 1859, Earl Cowper formed the Hertfordshire Rifle Volunteer Corps, which in 1877 became the Herts Rifle Volunteers. In 1900 the unit became associated with The Bedfordshire Regiment as its 1st (Herts) Volunteer Battalion, but it achieved a separate identity in 1909 when designated The Hertfordshire Regiment. About the same time the badge of Hertford, namely "A Hart lodged in Water," was adopted. The unit forms part of the corps of The Bedfordshire and Hertfordshire Regiment.

THE HEREFORDSHIRE LIGHT INFANTRY

Up to May, 1947, the title of the unit was "The Herefordshire Regiment", and its badge was a lion passant guardant standing on a wreath (straight) holding a sword, point uppermost, in its outstretched right paw; below the wreath a scroll inscribed "Herefordshire".

UNDER ARMY ORDER 67 of 1947 the title was changed to "The Herefordshire Light Infantry" consequent upon its becoming a unit of the Light Infantry Group, to which the parent corps, The King's Shropshire Light Infantry, also belongs. Owing to this the badge was altered to a bugle with strings thereon, the lion holding the sword as in the previous badge, standing on a tablet inscribed with the unit's motto "MANU FORTI." For officers the badge is in silver plate and for other ranks it is in white metal.

The old badge described in the first paragraph is to be retained as the collar badge: in silver plate for officers and in white metal with the scroll in gilding metal for other ranks.

The lion holding the sword comes from the Arms of Hereford. The city received its first charter from King Richard I (1189–1199), since when lions have appeared in its Arms. In 1645, as a Royalist stronghold, it was besieged by the Scots, and the sword commemorates its service to the Crown.

7TH AND 8TH BATTALIONS THE WEST YORKSHIRE REGIMENT

A star similar to the star of the Order of the Bath, thereon a circle inscribed "Leeds Rifles" and within the circle a bugle and crown; the star surmounted by a crown and all within a laurel wreath. On the lower portion of the wreath scrolls inscribed "7th 8th Bns. P.W.O. West Yorkshire Regt." Below the bottom arm of the star the battle honour "Tardenois" is inscribed. In silver for officers and black for other ranks.

THESE BATTALIONS had a common origin in the "Leeds Rifles," an unofficial name given to the unit raised in 1859. This unofficial title was later approved and incorporated into the official designation. For many years it was known as the 7th West Riding of Yorkshire, but at the time of the formation of the Territorial Force in 1908 it was the 3rd Volunteer Bn. The West Yorkshire

Regiment. On formation of the Territorial Force in 1908 it became 7th and 8th Battalions The West Yorkshire Regiment. Converted to an anti-aircraft role as 66th (Leeds Rifles) A.A. Brigade, R.A., in December, 1936, and since May, 1947, has been designated 466 (Leeds Rifles) (M.) H.A.A. Regiment, R.A. (T.A.).

Its original "Rifle" connection is maintained in the badge, which approximates that of The Rifle Brigade in design, except that it is black and not in silver.

5TH (CINQUE PORTS) BATTALION
THE ROYAL SUSSEX REGIMENT

A Maltese Cross, similar to that in the Order of the Bath but without the lions in the angles, in front of the Roussillon plume; in the centre of the cross a circle bearing on a shield the Arms of the Cinque Ports; below the cross a scroll inscribed "Cinque Ports". Other ranks' badge in gilding metal.

THE ARMS of the Cinque Ports were worn as a badge by the Cinque Ports Volunteers raised in 1859. The battalion has a long association with The Royal Sussex Regiment and bears its Roussillon plume. The original Cinque Ports are Hastings, Hythe, Dover, Romney and Sandwich, to which others have been added.

The badge was officially authorized in 1909. The Cinque Ports had military associations, in the form of Rifle Clubs, many years before 1859. In 1861 the Rifle Volunteer units of the Cinque Ports were formed into two Administrative Battalions, which in 1874 were resolved into one battalion. In 1881 the battalion was associated with The Royal Sussex Regiment but was permitted to have the Arms of the Cinque Ports with the Star and Roussillon plume as its badge, and on the formation of the Territorial Force in 1908 it was designated 5th (Cinque Ports) Bn. The Royal Sussex Regiment.

THE ROYAL HAMPSHIRE REGIMENT
6TH (DUKE OF CONNAUGHT'S OWN) BATTALION

OFFICERS

OTHER RANKS

Officers: The Hampshire Rose within a circle inscribed "Duke of Connaught's Own", the whole within a wreath of laurel and ensigned with the Duke's coronet; below the wreath a scroll inscribed "Hampshire" for other ranks. For other ranks the rose and scroll in gilding metal, the remainder in white metal.

THIS BATTALION traces its origin to certain Volunteer Companies raised in and about Portsmouth just after the middle of last century. In 1880 they became the 3rd Hampshire Rifle Volunteer Rifle Corps which later developed into the 3rd Volunteer Bn. The Hampshire Regiment. In 1903 H.R.H. The Duke of Connaught honoured the battalion by becoming its Honorary Colonel, an appointment he held until his death in January, 1942. "Duke of Connaught's Own" was added to its designation in

1903. On the formation of the Territorial Force in 1908 it became the 6th (Duke of Connaught's Own) Bn. The Hampshire Regiment. In 1937 it was converted to an artillery role as the 59th Anti-Tank Regiment, R.A., and today it is the 383 Anti-Tank Regiment, R.A. (T.A.), and now wears the Royal Artillery cap badge.

THE ROYAL HAMPSHIRE REGIMENT
7TH BATTALION

A "Stirrup" within a laurel wreath; on the lower portion of the wreath a scroll inscribed "7th Bn. Hampshire Regt."

THE "STIRRUP" has nothing to do with horse riding, but is a metal gauge in the shape of a stirrup, which was once used to measure dogs in the New Forest. At present it is chained to the wall in the old Verderers' Hall in The King's House at Lyndhurst. Traditionally, it is supposed to be King Rufus's stirrup and that any dog that could get through it had to be expeditated—that is, have the three middle claws of its front paws removed to prevent it from running fast enough to chase deer. The actual measurements are: From the "foot rest" to top of arch 6½ in., width of "foot rest" 9½ in. From this it will be seen that quite small dogs could not get through. The "stirrup" is, in fact, of early Tudor pattern. Under the Forest Laws no dogs were allowed in the Forest, but as in those days some of the Forest inhabitants were not "quite nice," people were allowed to keep a mastiff in the

Forest for personal protection, all of which had to be expeditated under the Lawing of Dogs. (I am indebted to D. W. Young, Esq., Deputy Surveyor, Forestry Commission, Lyndhurst, for these details of the "Stirrup."—T. J. E.)

On the re-forming of the Territorial Army after the Second World War, the role of the Regiment was changed and its present title is 524th Light Anti-Aircraft/Searchlight Regiment, Royal Artillery (7th Royal Hampshire Regiment).

It now wears the R.A. cap badge.

THE ROYAL HAMPSHIRE REGIMENT
8TH (THE PRINCESS BEATRICE'S ISLE OF WIGHT RIFLES) BATTALION

Carisbrooke Castle within a circle inscribed "Isle of Wight Rifles," within a wreath of laurel; above the circle a scroll inscribed "South Africa 1900–01", and below the circle a scroll inscribed "Princess Beatrice's"; the whole ensigned with a crown. The Princess Beatrice, the youngest daughter of Queen Victoria, was Honorary Colonel of this unit from 11th May, 1937, until her death on 26th October, 1944. H.R.H. was also Governor of the Isle of Wight and Carisbrooke Castle. In black metal.

THIS UNIT has had many changes in its official title since 1860, when it was the 1st Administrative Bn. Isle of Wight Volunteers. In 1880 it became the 1st Isle of Wight Volunteer Corps and in 1885 the 5th (Isle of Wight, Princess Beatrice's) Volunteer Bn. The Hampshire Regiment, the Princess being the wife of the late Prince Henry of Battenburg, who was Honorary Colonel of the unit. In 1897 H.R.H. The Duke of York, later King George V, honoured the Battalion by becoming its Honorary Colonel and retained the appointment until his death in 1936, when the Princess Beatrice succeeded him in the post. In 1908 it became the 8th Bn. The Hampshire Regiment, and in 1937 it was converted to an artillery role with the title "Princess Beatrice's (Isle of Wight Rifles) Heavy Brigade R.A. (T.A.)," but the following year it became a Coast Artillery Regiment. Its present title is 428 Heavy Anti-Aircraft Regiment, R.A. (T.A.), and it now wears the R.A. cap badge.

THE TYNESIDE SCOTTISH
670 L.A.A. REGIMENT, R.A. (T.A.)

St. Andrew's Cross; on the lower portion a tablet inscribed "Tyneside Scottish"; resting on the centre of the tablet and reaching to the centre of the cross, a tower, surmounted by the Scottish Lion bearing in its front paws a flagstaff carrying a swallow-tailed flag, in the centre of which is a small St. Andrew's Cross; sprays of thistle emerge from the tablet up each side of the cross. The badge is in white metal for all ranks.

THIS UNIT was formed in October, 1914, but recruiting was so favourable that a Tyneside Scottish Brigade of four battalions was formed in a short time, which became the 20th, 21st, 22nd and 23rd Bns. The Northumberland Fusiliers. Tyneside is represented in the badge by the tower from the Arms of Newcastle-on-Tyne. These battalions ceased to exist after the Great War. On the expansion of the T.A. in 1939 a duplicate battalion of the 9th Bn. The Durham Light Infantry became The Tyneside Scottish, but soon afterwards it was transferred to The Black Watch.

THE BUCKINGHAMSHIRE BATTALION, THE OXFORDSHIRE AND BUCKINGHAMSHIRE LIGHT INFANTRY

A Maltese Cross, thereon a circle inscribed "Buckingham-shire Battalion"; within the circle a Swan; the whole ensigned with a crown. In silver for officers and in black metal for other ranks.

THE SWAN in the centre of the badge is that used by the Buckinghamshire County Council and is derived from the White Swan of the Staffords, Dukes of Buckingham.

This unit was raised in 1860 as the 1st Buckinghamshire Rifle Volunteers and retained that title until becoming The Buckinghamshire Battalion, The Oxfordshire and Buckinghamshire Light Infantry in 1908. A detachment served with the parent Regular regiment in the Boer War, and the whole battalion gained further laurels in the Great War, 1914-1918. Its Reserve Battalion was designated 2nd/1st Bucks Battalion in September, 1914, but was usually referred to as the 2nd Bucks Battalion.

It also served with distinction in the Great War. Further honours fell to the Buckinghamshire Battalion as a result of service in the late war.

It was converted to R.A. when the Territorial Army was re-formed in 1947 and is now 645th Light Anti-Aircraft Regiment, Royal Artillery (Bucks), but it continues to wear the badge depicted.

7th (ROBIN HOODS) BATTALION
THE SHERWOOD FORESTERS

Design follows the model of The Rifle Brigade, being a cross as in the Order of the Bath, thereon a circle inscribed "The Robin Hoods" enclosing a bugle surmounted by a crown; the cross is enclosed in a laurel wreath and surmounted by a crown; the battle honour "South Africa 1900-02" is on three arms of the cross, viz. "South" on the left, "Africa" on the right, and "1900-02" on the bottom arm. In white metal for officers; other ranks in black.

THIS REGIMENT was formed in 1859 and was known in its early years as The Robin Hood Rifles. Its first parade took place on the Green at Nottingham Castle, and an engraved stone near the terrace doorway records the fact. During the war in South Africa at the beginning of the present century it sent contingents to the Cape, and "South Africa, 1900-02" on the badge commemorates this. On the formation of the Territorial Force in 1908 it became 7th Battalion The Sherwood Foresters, this being changed to 7th

(Robin Hood) Battalion a few years later. It served with distinction in the Great War, 1914-18. In December, 1936, it underwent a change of role and became the 42nd (Robin Hoods, Sherwood Foresters) A.A. Bn. R.E., but in August, 1940, it was transferred to the R.A. as the 42nd (Robin Hoods, Sherwood Foresters) Searchlight Regiment, R.A. It served again overseas in the late war, arriving in Normandy in 1944. Further changes of title took place, until finally it was designated 577 L.A.A./S.L. Regiment, R.A. (Robin Hoods, Foresters), T.A.

5TH BATTALION THE SEAFORTH HIGHLANDERS

A cat sitting on a scroll within a circle inscribed with the motto "Sans Peur" (Without fear). In gilding metal for other ranks.

THIS BATTALION had its origin in the Volunteer movement just after the middle of last century. It was raised by the Duke of Sutherland, whose crest of the Cat-a-Mountain, sejant, rampant, guardant, together with the motto "Sans Peur" (Without Fear) became the badge of the unit. Some years later the Caithness Volunteers were amalgamated with it, and the combined unit was designated 1st Sutherland Highland Rifle Volunteers. On the inauguration of the Territorial Force in 1908 it became the 5th (Sutherland and Caithness) Battalion The Seaforth Highlanders, but was permitted to retain the Sutherland badge. As a unit of the 51st Highland Division it fought with distinction in the Great War of 1914-18. In 1921 it was amalgamated with the 4th Battalion and re-designated 4th/5th Bn. The Seaforth Highlanders, and as such joined the B.E.F. in France at the outset of the late war. Later, however, it regained its old title of 5th (Caithness and Sutherland) Battalion and gathered further laurels during that campaign.

LIVERPOOL SCOTTISH

*St. Andrew within a wreath of thistles with two scrolls
inscribed "Liverpool Scottish" and a scroll under inscribed
"Cameron". The badge is in silver for officers and in white
metal for other ranks.*

THIS UNIT was raised from among Scotsmen in Liverpool in
April, 1900, at the time of the South African War, being designated the 8th (Scottish) Volunteer Battalion, The King's Liverpool Regiment. In 1908, when the Territorial Force was in-
augurated, it became the 10th (Scottish) Battalion The King's
(Liverpool) Regiment. Its badge was the St. Andrew's Cross,
thereon the White Horse below which was a scroll inscribed
"The King's": the whole within branches of thistle, prolonged
at the top by a scroll inscribed "Liverpool Scottish."

In 1937 (A.O. 189/1937) the unit was transferred to The
Queen's Own Cameron Highlanders and re-designated "The
Liverpool Scottish, The Queen's Own Cameron Highlanders"
(A.O. 195/1937) and the design of the badge changed, in con-
sequence, to approximate its new parent regular corps as above
depicted.

LONDON REGIMENTS

THE HISTORY of the Volunteer and Territorial Army units raised in and about London during 1859-60 has been quite different, in some respects, from that of similar units raised in the provinces. This has probably been due to the fact that London has only one Regular Infantry regiment, The Royal Fusiliers (City of London Regiment). Whilst other Infantry T.A. units could be brought within the organization of the County Regiment without any difficulty, the London units were not so conveniently situated. At one period they had practically an independent existence, and at another they were all grouped together into one Corps called "The London Regiment"; then later (1935-37) they were distributed among a number of Regular Corps, as at present. This has had its effect upon the badges worn at different periods of regimental history.

In the following statement the title of the unit and the cap badge worn at certain periods only is given, from the institution of the Territorial Force in 1908 (re-named Territorial Army, 1921) to the present day (1950). The period of World War II. 1939-1945, is omitted, it having been found that a variety of badges were worn in the same unit, some wearing their old pattern, others that of the Corps to which the unit had been converted, and in at least one unit a completely new and original (and unauthorized) badge was worn.

It is realized that a number of London units can trace their origin to military bodies which existed in their localities long before 1859-1860, some going back to the latter part of the eighteenth century; but 1859-1860 has been chosen here, because it is the general starting point of the present regiments.

1st CITY OF LONDON REGIMENT

A grenade, on the ball of which is the Garter ensigned with the crown, and within the Garter a rose. The mass of flames is roughly triangular in shape and the crown rests upon the "neck" between the flames and the ball. The badge is in bronze for officers, gilding metal for other ranks.

THIS UNIT was raised in 1860 as the 19th Middlesex Rifle Volunteers (Bloomsbury).

1908. 1st City of London Bn. (The Royal Fusiliers), The London Regiment.

1922. 1st City of London Regiment (The Royal Fusiliers), The London Regiment.

1937. 8th (1st City of London) Bn. The Royal Fusiliers (City of London Regiment).

1949. As in 1937.

This unit was a Volunteer battalion of The Royal Fusiliers before 1908, and it has always worn the badge of that regiment since then.

Note.—The sealed pattern now has a petal of the rose uppermost, and not the division between two petals as depicted.

A grenade, on the ball of which is the Garter ensigned with the crown, and within the Garter a rose. The mass of flames is roughly triangular in shape and the crown rests upon the "neck" between the flames and the ball. The badge is in bronze for officers, gilding metal for other ranks.

THIS UNIT was raised in 1860 as the 46th Middlesex Volunteer Rifle Corps.

    1908. 2nd City of London Bn. (The Royal Fusiliers), The London Regiment.

    1922. 2nd City of London Regiment (The Royal Fusiliers), The London Regiment.

    1937. 9th (2nd City of London) Bn. The Royal Fusiliers (City of London Regiment).

    1949. 624th Light Anti-Aircraft Regiment, R.A. (Royal Fusiliers).

This unit was a Volunteer battalion of The Royal Fusiliers before 1908, and it wore The Royal Fusiliers' badge from 1908 to 1948. In 1949, however, the badge of the Royal Artillery was adopted.

Note.—Sealed pattern as 1st City of London Regiment.

A grenade, on the ball of which is the Garter ensigned with the crown, and within the Garter a rose. The mass of flames is roughly triangular in shape and the crown rests upon the "neck" between the flames and the ball. The badge is in bronze for officers, gilding metal for other ranks.

THIS UNIT was raised in 1859 as the 20th Middlesex Rifle Volunteers.

    1908.   3rd City of London Battalion, (The Royal Fusiliers), The London Regiment.

    922.   3rd City of London Regiment (The Royal Fusiliers), The London Regiment.

    1937.   10th (3rd City of London) Bn. The Royal Fusiliers (City of London Regiment).

    1949.   625th Light Anti-Aircraft Regiment, R.A. (Royal Fusiliers).

This unit was a Volunteer battalion of The Royal Fusiliers before 1908 and has worn The Royal Fusiliers' badge ever since that time, and still continues to wear it, though a unit of the R.A.

Note.—Sealed pattern as 1st City of London Regiment.

4TH CITY OF LONDON REGIMENT

A grenade, on the ball of which is the Garter ensigned with the crown, and within the Garter a rose. The mass of flames is roughly triangular in shape and the crown rests upon the "neck" between the flames and the ball. The badge is in bronze for officers, gilding metal for other ranks.

THIS UNIT was raised in 1860 as the Tower Hamlets Rifle Volunteers.

    1908.   4th City of London Battalion (The Royal Fusiliers), The London Regiment.

    1922.   4th City of London Regiment (The Royal Fusiliers) The London Regiment.

    1936.   60th (City of London) Anti-Aircraft Brigade, R.A.

    1949.   460th Heavy Anti-Aircraft Regiment, R.A. (City of London).

This unit was a Volunteer battalion of The Royal Fusiliers before 1908, and wore the badge of that regiment until converted to a brigade of R.A. in 1936, since when the R.A. badge has been worn.

Note.—Sealed pattern as 1st City of London Regiment.

Their cap badge is The Royal Arms on a shield within a circle inscribed in the upper portion "London Rifle Brigade" and in the lower portion with the battle honour "South Africa 1900-02"; immediately above the circle, a scroll inscribed with the battle honour "France & Flanders 1914-18", and immediately below the circle another scroll inscribed with the battle honour "Ypres 1915, '17"; the circle and shield are on the City Sword and Mace and enclosed in an oak wreath which bears scrolls inscribed with four other battle honours on each side; below the scroll inscribed "Ypres 1915, '17" is another scroll inscribed "Primus in Urbe" (First in the City), and below this latter scroll an escutcheon of the Arms of the City of London (i.e., a silver shield bearing a cross, in the first quarter a sword erect with point upwards); a crown surmounts the whole. The badge is in white metal.

THIS UNIT was raised in 1859 as the 1st City of London Volunteer Rifle Brigade.

1908.   5th City of London Bn. The London Regiment.

1922.   5th City of London Regiment (London Rifle Brigade), The London Regiment.

1937.   London Rifle Brigade, The Rifle Brigade (Prince Consort's Own).

1949.   7th Bn. The Rifle Brigade (Prince Consort's Own) (London Rifle Brigade).

The Royal Arms are in allusion to H.R.H. The Duke of Cambridge, who was Honorary Colonel of the regiment from 1860 to his death in 1904. The motto refers to the fact that the unit was the first to be raised in the City of London in 1859, and the Sword, Mace and Arms of the city are also linked to London. Being a Rifle regiment it does not carry Colours, hence some of its battle honours are inscribed on the badge.

From 1908 until 1935 the badge was a Maltese Cross, in the centre of which a circle inscribed "6th Battn. City of London Regt.", a bugle within the circle; above, and resting on the top arm of the cross, a tablet inscribed with the motto of the City of London, viz. "Domine Dirige Nos" (Lord, direct us), surmounted by a crown; in the top arm of the cross the battle honour "South Africa 1900–02" is inscribed.

THIS UNIT was raised in 1860 as the 2nd London Volunteer Rifle Corps.

 1908. 6th Bn. The London Regiment (City of London Rifles).

 1935. 31st (City of London Rifles) Anti-Aircraft Bn. R.E.

 1940. 31st (City of London) Searchlight Regiment, R.A.

 1949. 566th L. A.A. Regt., R.A. (City of London Rifles).

    674th H. A.A. Regt., R.A. (City of London Rifles).

The badge of the Royal Engineers was adopted on conversion in 1935, and that of the Royal Artillery when transferred to that Corps in 1940, the latter badge still being worn.

The badge of the 7th between 1908 and 1922 was a grenade with the arabic figure "7" on the ball. The badge of the 8th from 1908 until 1935 was of The Rifle Brigade pattern, being a Maltese Cross, on the top arm of which was a tablet inscribed "8th Battalion", surmounted by a crown; below the cross, a scroll inscribed "City of London"; in the centre a circle inscribed "Post Office Rifles"; a laurel wreath encircled the badge, upon which was inscribed the battle honours "Egypt 1882" and "South Africa 1899-02". The battle honour "Egypt 1882" is unique among non-Regular army units, and it was granted to the Post Office Rifles to commemorate service of their members who volunteered for duty with the Cable and Telegraph Companies of the R.E. during the Egyptian Campaign of 1882.

THE 7TH was raised in 1859 as the 3rd London Volunteer Rifle Corps.

1908.   7th (City of London) Bn. The London Regiment.

1921.   7th (City of London) Bn. The London Regiment (The Royal Fusiliers).

1922.   Amalgamated with 8th Battalion. See below.

        The 8th was raised in 1868 as the 49th Middlesex Rifle Volunteer Corps.

1908.   8th (City of London) Bn. The London Regiment (Post Office Rifles).

1922.   Amalgamated with 7th Battalion. See below.

The 7th and 8th were amalgamated in 1922 under the title 7th City of London Regiment (Post Office Rifles). In 1935 the new unit was converted to the 32nd (7th City of London) Anti-Aircraft Bn. Royal Engineers, and is now the 567th (M.) L.A.A./S.L. Regiment, R.A. (City of London).

Since conversion to R.A. in 1939 the R.A. badge has been worn.

*The badge is similar in design to that of the K.R.R.C.,
being a Maltese Cross with a circle in the centre inscribed
"Queen Victoria's" enclosing St. George killing the
Dragon; above, and resting on the top arm of the cross, a
tablet inscribed "South Africa 1900–02" with a crown
above. The central feature of St. George killing the
Dragon commemorates the old St. George's Volunteer
Rifle Corps.*

THIS UNIT was raised in 1859 as the 1st Middlesex Rifle Volunteers
(Victoria Volunteer Rifle Corps) and the 11th Middlesex Rifle
Volunteers (St. George's Volunteer Rifle Corps), the two units
being amalgamated in 1892 as The Victoria and St. George's
Rifles (1st Volunteer Bn. The K.R.R.C.).

- 1908. 9th Bn. County of London (Queen Victoria's) The
London Regiment.
- 1922. 9th London Regiment (Queen Victoria's Rifles).
- 1937. Queen Victoria's Rifles, The King's Royal Rifle Corps.
- 1949. 7th Bn. The King's Royal Rifle Corps (Queen Victoria's Rifles).

From 1913 until 1937 the unit wore its own badge, viz.
a laurel wreath, thereon an eight-pointed star, the topmost
point displaced by a crown; in the centre a circle inscribed
"Justitia Turris Nostra" (Justice is our tower), and within
the circle a tower as in the seal of the Borough of Hackney;
below the lower portion of the wreath a scroll inscribed
"Tenth London Hackney".

THIS UNIT was raised in 1912 as the 10th (County of London) Bn.
The London Regiment.

1912.   10th (County of London) Bn. The London Regiment
(Hackney).

1922.   10th London Regiment (Hackney).

1937.   5th (Hackney) Bn. The Royal Berkshire Regiment
(Princess Charlotte of Wales's).

1949.   648th Heavy Anti-Aircraft Regiment, R.A. (Royal
Berkshire).

Since 1937, when the unit became a battalion of The Royal
Berkshire Regiment, the badge of that regiment has been worn
and is still worn, although it is now a unit of the R.A.

Until converted to an R.A. unit in 1936 the badge worn was a Maltese Cross, in the centre a circle inscribed "Finsbury Rifles" enclosing a bugle; above, and resting on the uppermost arm of the cross, a tablet inscribed "South Africa 1900-02" with a crown above; the motto "Pro Aris et Focis" (For our altars and our hearths) is inscribed on the arms of the cross.

THIS UNIT was raised in 1859 as the 39th Middlesex Rifle Volunteer Corps, and four years later was known as The Finsbury Rifles.

1908. 11th (County of London) Bn. The London Regiment (Finsbury Rifles).

1922. 11th London Regiment (Finsbury Rifles).

1936. 61st (Finsbury Rifles) Anti-Aircraft Brigade, R.A.

1949. 461st Heavy Anti-Aircraft Regiment, R.A. (Middlesex).

Since conversion the R.A. badge has been worn.

Up to 1948, during which period the unit was associated with The King's Royal Rifle Corps, the badge was modelled on that of the K.R.R.C., being a Maltese Cross, in the centre of which a circle inscribed "The King's Royal Rifle Corps" enclosing a bugle; above the top arm of the cross, a crown; battle honours inscribed on each arm of the cross; below the cross, a scroll inscribed "The Rangers". Since the unit was transferred from the K.R.R.C. to The Rifle Brigade, the only change in the badge is to substitute "The Rifle Brigade" on the circle in the centre.

THIS UNIT was raised in 1860 as the 40th Middlesex Rifle Volunteers (Gray's Inn).

- 1908.   12th (County of London) Bn. The London Regiment (The Rangers).
- 1922.   12th London Regiment (Rangers).
- 1937.   The Rangers, The King's Royal Rifle Corps.
- 1949.   The Rangers, The Rifle Brigade (Prince Consort's Own).

The Arms of the Royal Borough of Kensington on an eight-pointed star. The Arms of Kensington are a shield with red and gold quarters within a border quartered gold and black; in the first quarter a celestial crown above a gold fleur-de-lis, and in the dexter chief point a five-pointed silver star; in the second a black cross flory and four black martlets; in the third a red cross bottony and four red roses with stems and leaves in natural colours; and in the fourth a gold mitre.

THIS UNIT was raised in 1859 as the 4th Middlesex (West London) Rifle Volunteers.

1908.   13th (County of London) Bn. The London Regiment (Kensington).

1922.   13th London Regt. (Princess Louise's Kensington Regt.).

1937.   Princess Louise's Kensington Regiment, The Middlesex Regiment (Duke of Cambridge's Own).

1949.   Army Phantom Signal Regiment (Princess Louise's Kensington Regiment).

The badge is St. Andrew's Cross, upon which is super-imposed the Lion of Scotland, the whole upon a circle inscribed "Strike Sure"; on the lowest portion of the circle is inscribed "S. Africa 1900–02"; on the top of the cross a scroll inscribed "London" and on the bottom a scroll inscribed "Scottish"; a wreath of thistles surrounds the whole.

THIS UNIT was raised in 1859 from amongst Scotsmen in London, and it was designated the 15th Middlesex (London Scottish) Rifle Volunteers.

    1908.   14th (County of London) Bn. The London Regiment (London Scottish).

    1922.   14th London Regiment (London Scottish).

    1937.   The London Scottish, The Gordon Highlanders.

    1949.   The London Scottish, The Gordon Highlanders.

The badge is a Maltese Cross surmounted by a crown; battle honours are on the arms of the cross; in the centre of the cross are two oval escutcheons, the left one bearing a portcullis (the Arms of Westminster) and the right one, which overlaps the left, bearing the Prince of Wales's plume of the Civil Service Rifles; a crown surmounts the whole.

THE 15TH was raised in 1859 as the 21st Middlesex (Civil Service) Rifle Volunteer Corps. It was amalgamated with the 16th in December, 1921. Its badge was the Prince of Wales's plume and was derived from its title of 15th (County of London) Bn. The London Regiment (Prince of Wales's Own, Civil Service Rifles). The Prince of Wales, later King Edward VII, was Honorary Colonel of the regiment, as also was the Duke of Windsor when Prince of Wales.

The 16th was raised in 1859 as the 22nd Middlesex (Queen's) Rifle Volunteers (Westminster).

1908. 16th (County of London) Bn. The London Regiment (Queen's Westminster Rifles).

1922. 16th London Regiment (Queen's Westminster and Civil Service Rifles).

1937. The Queen's Westminsters, The King's Royal Rifle Corps.

1949. The Queen's Westminsters, The King's Royal Rifle Corps.

Until 1947 a badge very similar in design to that of The Rifle Brigade was worn, being: the cross as in the Order of the Bath, thereon a circle inscribed "Tower Hamlets Rifles —The Rifle Brigade", enclosing a bugle with crown above; above the cross a tablet inscribed "South Africa, 1900-02", surmounted by a crown; the whole within a laurel wreath bearing scrolls inscribed with battle honours; on the lower portion of the wreath a scroll inscribed "Prince Consort's Own"; battle honours are also on the arms of the cross.

THIS UNIT was raised in 1859 as the 26th Middlesex Rifle Volunteers.

1908. 17th (County of London) Bn. The London Regiment (Poplar and Stepney Rifles).

1922. 17th London Regiment (Poplar and Stepney Rifles).

1937. Tower Hamlets Rifles, The Rifle Brigade.

1949. 656th Light Anti-Aircraft Regiment, R.A. (Rifle Brigade).

Since being constituted an R.A. unit the R.A. badge has been worn.

The badge is the Irish Harp surmounted by a crown, and it will be noticed that, unlike all other Irish regiments, this is the only one existing with the original Irish Harp without the Maid of Erin.

THIS UNIT was raised in 1859 as the 28th Middlesex (London Irish) Rifle Volunteers, being recruited from among Irishmen in London.

1908. 18th (County of London) Bn. The London Regiment (London Irish Rifles).

1922. 18th London Regiment (London Irish Rifles).

1937. London Irish Rifles, The Royal Ulster Rifles.

1949. London Irish Rifles, The Royal Ulster Rifles.

This unit wore a badge similar to that of The Rifle Brigade up to the time it was converted to R.E. in 1936. The badge was the cross as in the Order of the Bath, surmounted by a crown; in the centre a circle inscribed "County of London—St. Pancras", and within the circle the Roman numeral "XIX"; on the top arm of the cross is "South Africa" and on the bottom "1900-02"; the whole enclosed in a laurel wreath.

THIS UNIT was raised in 1859 as the 29th (North) Middlesex Rifle Volunteers.

1908.   19th (County of London) Bn. The London Regiment (St. Pancras).

1922.   19th London Regiment (St. Pancras).

1936.   33rd (St. Pancras) Anti-Aircraft Bn. Royal Engineers.

1949.   568th (St. Pancras) (M.) L.A.A./S.L. Regiment, R.A.

On conversion to R.E. the R.E. badge was worn, and again on conversion to R.A. in 1940 the R.A. badge was worn.

The badge worn now, as always, is the White Horse of Kent standing on a scroll inscribed in Old English "Invicta" (Unconquered), below which is another scroll inscribed "20th Batt. The London Regiment". In white metal for other ranks, and for officers the Horse in silver plate and the remainder in gilt.

THIS UNIT was raised in 1859 as the 3rd and 4th Kent Rifle Volunteers, being subsequently amalgamated to form one unit.

    1908.   20th (County of London) Bn. The London Regiment (Blackheath and Woolwich).

    1922.   20th London Regiment (The Queen's Own).

    1936.   34th (The Queen's Own Royal West Kent) Anti-Aircraft Bn., R.E.

    1949.   569th (M.) L.A.A./S.L. Regiment, R.A. (Queen's Own Royal West Kent).

*Until 1935 the unit wore a badge of Rifle pattern, being a
cross as in the Order of the Bath, thereon a circle inscribed
"First Surrey Rifles" enclosing a bugle; within the top
arm is "South Africa 1900-02" and above the arm a
scroll inscribed "Concordia Victrix" (A good spirit (friend-
ship) conquers), surmounted by a crown; below the cross a
scroll inscribed "21st County of London".*

THIS UNIT was raised in 1859 as the 1st Surrey Rifle Volunteers.

    1908.   21st (County of London) Bn. The London Regiment
             (First Surrey Rifles).

    1922.   21st London Regiment (First Surrey Rifles).

    1935.   35th (First Surrey Rifles) Anti-Aircraft Bn. R.E.

    1949.   570th L.A.A. Regt., R.A. (First Surrey Rifles).

After conversion to R.E. it adopted the R.E. badge, and on
being transferred to R.A. in 1940 the R.A. badge was worn,
but in 1947 it re-adopted the above badge, in black metal,
for other ranks, the officers and warrant officers wearing the red
boss with a silver stringed bugle.

The Paschal Lamb. The badge is in frosted gilt or gilding metal for officers and gilding metal for other ranks.

THIS UNIT was raised in 1859 as the 6th Surrey Rifle Volunteer Corps.

1908. 22nd (County of London) Bn. The London Regiment (The Queen's).

1922. 22nd London Regiment (The Queen's).

1937. 6th (Bermondsey) Bn. The Queen's Royal Regiment (West Surrey).

1949. As in 1937.

This unit has a long association with The Queen's Royal Regiment (West Surrey) and wears the badge of that Corps, viz. the Paschal Lamb.

Up to the time this unit was converted to a unit of The Royal Tank Regiment in 1939 it wore a badge modelled upon that of The East Surrey Regiment, being an eight-pointed star, the topmost point displaced by a crown; on the star a circle inscribed "South Africa 1900-02", and within the circle the Arms of Guildford; below the star a scroll inscribed "23rd Bn. The London Regt."

THIS UNIT originated in 1859 as the 7th and 26th Surrey Rifle Volunteer Corps, which were amalgamated in 1880.

    1908.   23rd (County of London) Bn. The London Regiment.

    1922.   23rd London Regiment.

    1937.   7th (23rd London) Bn. The East Surrey Regiment.

    1949.   42nd Bn. Royal Tank Regiment, R.A.C.

On conversion to the R.T.R. the badge of that regiment was adopted.

The Paschal Lamb. The badge is in frosted gilt or gilding metal for officers and gilding metal for other ranks.

THIS UNIT was raised in 1859 as the 8th Surrey Rifle Volunteer Corps.

    1908.   24th (County of London) Bn. The London Regiment (The Queen's).

    1922.   24th London Regiment (The Queen's).

    1937.   7th (Southwark) Bn. The Queen's Royal Regiment (West Surrey).

    1949.   622nd Heavy Anti-Aircraft Regiment, R.A. (Queen's).

Although this unit has been converted to the R.A., the Paschal Lamb badge of The Queen's is still worn.

Its badge was a cycle wheel inscribed in the centre with the arabic numeral "25" within a circle inscribed "County of London Cyclists", the circle within a laurel wreath, the whole surmounted by a crown; below the wheel a tablet inscribed "Tenax et Audax" (Tenacious and Bold).

THIS UNIT was raised in 1888 as the 26th Middlesex Volunteer Rifle Corps. In 1908 its title was 25th (County of London) Cyclist Bn. The London Regiment. It was disbanded in 1922.

During its short existence it was the only complete unit in the Army entirely equipped with cycles, although other units had a proportion of their strength so mounted. Volunteers of the unit served in the South African War, 1899-1902, with the City Imperial Volunteers, but during the Great War of 1914-1918 it raised three battalions and gained honours for service in Waziristan in 1917 and for the Third Afghan War (Afghanistan, 1919). Drafts from the unit also served in Mesopotamia and France.

ROYAL ARMY CHAPLAINS'
DEPARTMENT

The Royal Army Chaplains' Department has two badges, one for Christians and the other for Jews. The badge for Christians is a Maltese Cross in silver, in the centre a circle inscribed "In This Sign Conquer" in gilt; within the circle in gilt a quatrefoil voided; the ground of the motto circle and quatrefoil is in blue enamel. The whole within a wreath in gilt, the right branch being of oak and the left of laurel; the whole surmounted by a crown in gilt. The badge for Jews is the Star of David, in the centre of which is a circle containing a quatrefoil within a laurel and oak wreath as in the badge for Christian Chaplains; a crown surmounts the whole badge. This badge, which is in black metal, was authorized by Army Order 124 of 1940.

IN THE badge for Christian Chaplains the cross and motto go together. In the wreath the branch of oak represents religious glory, and the laurel denotes a military association.

Jewish Chaplains wear a badge of the Star of David—a double triangle intertwined.

Chaplains were first commissioned in the Army in 1662, the year in which Parliament accepted the Reformed Prayer Book.

The present Royal Army Chaplains' Department was formed in November, 1858. It then consisted of 20 Staff Chaplains and 35 Assistant Chaplains, all belonging to the Church of England, who were paid under the Chaplains Warrant of 1847.

In the revised Warrant of 1858, 19 Roman Catholic priests and 5 Presbyterian ministers were added to the establishment. Roman Catholics and Presbyterians had been paid as Acting Chaplains since 1836, but this is the first occasion of Chaplains of denominations other than the Church of England being granted commissions.

ROYAL ARMY SERVICE CORPS

An eight-pointed star, the topmost point displaced by a crown; on the star a laurel wreath bearing a scroll inscribed "Royal Army Service Corps"; within the wreath the Garter and motto; and within the Garter the Royal Cypher. For officers the star and crown are in chromium-plated finish; the Garter and motto is on flush blue enamel ground; the Royal Cypher is backed with red enamel; the remainder of the badge is in gilt. For other ranks the badge is in gilding metal.

THE STAR, crown and Garter are similar to those previously worn on the helmet plate; the Royal Cypher was worn on the buttons of the Army Service Corps and is changed with succeeding Sovereigns. The Corps was granted Royal in 1918 (A.O. 362/1918) in recognition of services during the Great War of 1914-18.

Early transport and supply arrangements were usually improvised by Commanders of Forces, but in 1794 a Corps of Waggoners was formed which five years later gave place to the Royal Wagon Train, this being disbanded in 1833. For the Crimean War a Land Transport Corps was formed which became the Military Train. The present corps finds a firm foundation in 1870 when the first Army Service Corps was formed, but split up into two separate corps in 1881. The present Corps dates from 1889.

The rod of Æsculapius with a serpent twined round it, head uppermost, within a wreath of laurel; the whole ensigned with a crown; below the wreath a scroll inscribed "In Arduis Fidelis", the Corps motto. For Officers the wreath, crown and rod are in gilt, the remainder in silver plate. Corresponding metals for other ranks.

ÆSCULAPIUS WAS the Greek god of medicine. The Royal Army Medical Corps was formed in 1898 by amalgamating the Medical Staff (officers) and the Medical Staff Corps (men) (Army Order 93 of 1898), and was granted the motto appearing on the scroll.

This badge was approved in May, 1902.

Before the establishment of the present standing army in 1661 doctors from civil life accompanied the troops on active service, returning to their practices at the end of hostilities. For a long time after 1661 medical officers were of a purely regimental character, and it was not until the Crimean War that they began to be organized. In 1857 the Army Hospital Corps was formed, and this became the Medical Staff Corps in 1884.

The R.A.O.C. have had three badges within recent years, viz.: (a) Up to March, 1947: *Within the Garter with its motto, the Shield of the Arms of the Board of Ordnance (i.e., three cannon balls in a row at the top of the Shield and three old muzzle-loading cannon, one above the other, in the remaining portion below); on a scroll below the Garter is inscribed "Royal Army Ordnance Corps"; the whole surmounted by a crown.* (b) From March, 1947, to November, 1949: *A badge of the same design as in* (a) *above, with the exception that on the scroll below the Garter, instead of the Corps title, is inscribed the Corps motto "Sua Tela Tonanti" (Of Jupiter—"Thundering forth his weapons"). The officers' badges were in gilt and silver, the Shield of Arms of the Board of Ordnance on a ground of blue. The badges for other ranks were in gilding metal.* (c) Since November, 1949: *The Shield of the Arms of the Board of Ordnance within the Garter, sur-*

mounted by a crown which comes down and rests upon the lower edge of the Garter; below the Garter a scroll inscribed "Sua Tela Tonanti". The officers' badges are as follows—the shield is in silver plate, and the Garter and crown in gilt; for other ranks the corresponding metals are gilding metal and white metal.

THE OLD Board of Ordnance originated in the fourteenth century and ceased to exist in 1855, when its duties were transferred to the Secretary of State for War. As the functions of the R.A.O.C. were analogous to those of the Board, it was natural that it should include the Arms of the Board in its badge. The motto is most appropriate as its duties are so closely concerned with weapons of all kinds.

ROYAL ELECTRICAL AND
MECHANICAL ENGINEERS

R.E.M.E. was formed in October, 1942, and the badge adopted was four shields, each bearing one of the initials of the Corps title placed on a laurel wreath in the form of a cross, with a pair of calipers in the centre and a crown above all. In July, 1947, a new badge was adopted—viz., a horse forcene (i.e., in a rearing attitude) with a coronet of four fleurs-de-lis round its neck, a chain attached to the coronet over its back, standing on a globe; above the horse a scroll inscribed "R.E.M.E" surmounted by a crown; the horse is upon a flash of lightning. For officers the horse and globe are in silver plate and the remainder in gilt; for other ranks the badge is in gilding and white metal.

THE HORSE with its chain symbolizes power under control, and the globe symbolizes the world-wide character of mechanical engineering. The lightning flash is emblematic of electrical engineering.

The badge is based upon that of the Institution of Mechanical Engineers (which includes the horse forcene, with coronet and chain standing upon a globe) with the flash of lightning, crown and scroll bearing R.E.M.E. added.

The Royal Cypher "GR VI" with crown above within a wreath of laurel; below the wreath a scroll inscribed "Royal Military Police". For officers it is in silver-plated metal and for other ranks in gilding metal.

THE PROVOST MARSHAL existed as far back as the fifteenth century, being assisted by "Provost Men." In Henry VIII's Articles of War of 1513 provision was made for a Provost Company. In 1855 twelve N.C.Os. from Cavalry Regiments performed duties as Mounted Police, but during the next twenty years a substantial increase in numbers was made and the Military Mounted Police was formed. The Military Foot Police was formed in 1885, and both the Mounted and Foot elements were amalgamated in 1926 to form the Corps of Military Police, being granted "Royal" in 1946 in recognition of their past services. The Corps is recruited from Regular Warrant Officers and N.C.Os. who fulfil the high physical, educational and moral standards required. Selected National Service personnel are also transferred to the Corps. The main duties of the Corps are the maintenance of discipline, traffic control in the field, and the prevention, detection and investigation of serious crime.

ROYAL ARMY PAY CORPS

The Royal Crest, i.e., Lion on the crown, over a scroll inscribed with the Corps motto "Fide et Fiducia" (In faith and trust). For officers the Royal Crest is gilt and the scroll is silver plate; for other ranks the Royal Crest is in gilding metal and the scroll is in white metal.

THE ROYAL CREST was a badge of the old Army Pay Department, which was amalgamated with the Army Pay Corps in 1920 (A.O. 146 of 1920) to form the present Corps.

The motto was granted under Army Order 175 of 1929.

During the Peninsular War the paymasters were on a regimental basis and had great difficulty in transporting their boxes all over Spain and Portugal. When service became somewhat hazardous and great speed was required, the boxes containing the money had to be thrown away, as was done during Sir John Moore's famous retreat to Corunna. From time to time pay arrangements have been modernized, and now we have a highly efficient corps which handles all the business of pay, allowances, allotments to families, and all the multiplicity of cash transactions involving serving personnel and those on the reserve as well as a certain amount of work connected with pensions.

*A Centaur within a wreath with crown above; below the
wreath a scroll inscribed "Royal Army Veterinary Corps".
In gilt for officers and gilding metal for other ranks.*

THE CENTAUR, a man with a horse's body and legs, is Chiron
(or Cheiron) of Greek mythology and typifies the role of the
Corps in providing the Army with horses under the direction of
man. The Army Veterinary Corps was granted "Royal" under
Army Order 362 of 1918, in recognition of its services during
the Great War of 1914-1918; hence the inscription on the scroll.

Up to quite modern times the horse was an important factor
in war, not only for the Cavalry arm but also for Artillery,
supplies and practically every form of transport. In the "days of
long ago" there was a "Martiall to ye Horse," and in the
eighteenth century each squadron of Cavalry had its farrier. It
was not, however, until 1858 that a Veterinary Medical Department was formed, and its successor was amalgamated with the
Army Veterinary Corps (formed in 1903 and composed of men
only) in 1906. Although the horse has in recent years given way
to mechanization, much of the success of our previous campaigns
was due to the unremitting care devoted to the horses by
Veterinary officers and farriers.

317

*A Vickers Machine Gun, thereon a pair of crossed rifles
with bayonets fixed, a crown within the angle formed by
the rifles above the machine gun; the whole within a laurel
wreath; on the wreath scrolls inscribed—on the left side
"Small", on the bottom "Arms", and on the right side
"School". In brass.*

THE CROSSED rifles with crown above was the original badge of
the School of Musketry formed in 1854, and was worn up to
1919, when the School became Small Arms School, Hythe. In
1923 it was amalgamated with the Machine Gun School,
Netheravon, which is represented by the machine gun in the
badge. In 1929 the amalgamated schools were formed into a
Corps and designated "Small Arms School Corps."

The Royal Cypher surmounted by a crown.

THE MILITARY PRISON STAFF CORPS was formed under A.O. 241 of 1901, being re-designated Military Provost Staff Corps in 1906.

Recruitment to the Corps is by the transfer of suitable N.C.Os., not below the rank of sergeant, from other regiments and corps. N.C.Os. of the Corps form the other-rank staff of Detention Barracks and similar units. Their primary duty is the re-training of a bad soldier as a good one.

ROYAL ARMY EDUCATIONAL CORPS

*A fluted flambeau of five flames (the emblem of learning),
thereon a crown, and below the crown a scroll inscribed
"R.A.E.C." For officers the crown and scroll are gilt and
the torch in silver plate; for other ranks the corresponding
metals are white metal and gilding metal.*

THIS BADGE was approved in 1950: the original badge worn
previously was an open book upon crossed lances and rifles with
a scroll below inscribed "Army Educational Corps."

Elements of a system of army education can be traced to the
eighteenth century, and early in the next century Sergeant-
Schoolmasters were appointed, and from these the Corps of
Army Schoolmasters developed. With the introduction of the
present multiplicity of weapons a higher standard of education
was required of the soldier to use them effectively, and to meet
this need the Army Educational Corps was formed in 1920 and
the Corps of Army Schoolmasters disbanded, a number of whose
members passed into the new Corps. In 1946 the A.E.C. was
granted the title "Royal," hence "R.A.E.C." on the scroll of
of the new badge.

ROYAL ARMY DENTAL CORPS

A Dragon's head, with a sword, hilt to the north east, in the Dragon's mouth, within a laurel wreath; above the Dragon, a crown; on the lower portion of the wreath a scroll inscribed with the Corps motto, "Ex Dentibus Ensis" (From the teeth a sword). For officers in gilt and silver; for other ranks in gilding metal.

THE CHINESE emblem of dentistry is the Dragon. In Greek mythology Cadmus, son of Agenor, King of Phœnicia, slew a dragon that had killed his companions. On instructions from Athena he sowed the dragon's teeth in the ground, and a race of fierce men sprang up called Sparti (Sown). Jason, too, sowed dragons' teeth from which armed men sprang up.

The Army Dental Corps was formed in 1921 (A.O. 4/1921), but throughout the Great War of 1914-1918 Dental officers had been on the establishment of all medical units. During the late war, owing to the work of the Corps, great numbers of men were made available for military service and also retained in the Army. The units that dealt specially with fractures of the jaw performed most valuable service. In recognition of their services the Corps was granted the title "Royal" in 1946 (A.O. 167/1946).

A "pile" consisting of a pick placed centrally, with a rifle crossing it in front from the left and a shovel crossing it between the rifle and pick from the right; on the pile a laurel wreath pointing downwards; above the pile a crown, and below, a scroll inscribed "Labor Omnia Vincit" (Labour conquers all things). For officers the badge is silver plated; for other ranks it is in gilding metal.

THE PICK and shovel are representative of the working aspect of the Corps, whilst the rifle symbolizes the fighting aspect. The laurel wreath denotes military fame achieved by giving expression to the motto.

A somewhat similar organization, the "Labour Corps," was formed during the Great War, 1914-1918, and possibly its existence suggested the raising of the Royal Pioneer Corps in October, 1939, whose designation then was "Auxiliary Military Pioneer Corps," shortened to "Pioneer Corps" under A.O. 200/1940. The Pioneer Corps differed from the Labour Corps in that it was fully combatant and performed excellent service in the operations leading to Dunkirk and subsequently on all fronts in the late war, for which it was granted the title "Royal" (A.O. 176/1946). Its first Colonel Commandant was the late Field-Marshal Lord Milne, to whose wise guidance in its early days are attributed many of its solid achievements.

INTELLIGENCE CORPS

A rose within two branches of laurel surmounted by a crown; below the laurel a scroll inscribed "Intelligence Corps". In silver plate for officers and gilding metal for other ranks.

THE ROSE is the emblem of secrecy, and is therefore most appropriate as a badge for this Corps, which was formed in July, 1940.

Before the outbreak of the late war intelligence appointments on the various Army staffs were filled by officers of the Regular Army Reserve of Officers who had been registered for these duties. The numbers, however, were few and it was with some difficulty that the requirements of the B.E.F. in France were met. Arrangements were therefore made for greatly increasing the numbers trained for such duties, but the increase in numbers resulted in the increased complexity of administration, a problem that was solved by incorporating all intelligence personnel into an Intelligence Corps (A.O. 112 of 1940). This new corps absorbed personnel employed on censor work and the Field Security Police.

Crossed swords surmounted by a crown. In bronze for officers and gilding metal for other ranks.

CROSSED SWORDS was the badge of Army Physical Training Staff long before the Army School of Physical Training became the Army Physical Training Corps in September, 1940.

The barred red and black jersey of the Army Physical Training Staff and the qualified unit instructors was a familiar article for many years before the formation of the A.P.T.C. The great demand for physical training instructors soon after the outbreak of the late war created the need for the efficient centralized administration of all personnel of the Army Physical Training Staff which led to the formation of the Army Physical Training Corps.

ARMY CATERING CORPS

An ancient Grecian brazier within a circle inscribed "Army Catering Corps", the circle surmounted by a crown. For officers the brazier is silver plated and the remainder gilt; for other ranks the badge is in gilding metal.

THE GRECIAN brazier symbolizes the art of cooking, which is a main duty of this Corps.

An Army School of Cookery had been established at Aldershot many years before the outbreak of the late war and was well known for its specialized training in the culinary art. With the great expansion of the Army in 1939 and a few years later, not only were more cooks required but expert advice was also needed in catering and cooking. Consequently it was decided to gather all unit cooks into one Corps which could control their training, administration and economical distribution throughout the Army wherever a unit may be serving. This Corps was formed under Army Order 35/1941 in March, 1941, as the Army Catering Corps.

*The Royal Crest upon crossed swords, points uppermost
(i.e., the Army Badge) below the crown the motto
"Deus Vult" on a scroll, and below this the emblems of
the countries of the United Kingdom—viz. Rose, Thistle,
Leek and Shamrock.*

THE G.S.C. was formed in February, 1942 (A.O. 19/1942) to
provide a "pool" into which enlisted men were first placed to
undergo selection tests to ascertain the most suitable arm in which
they should serve. Although still in being, the functions of the
Corps have been modified.

HIGH COMMISSION TERRITORIES CORPS

*On a solid centre the monogram "HCT" within a wreath
of laurel, surmounted by a crown; below the wreath a
scroll inscribed "Basutoland", or "Bechuanaland", or
"Swaziland", according to the country to which personnel
belong. The badge is in gilding metal.*

THE HIGH COMMISSION TERRITORIES CORPS was raised in June, 1942,
as the "African Auxiliary Pioneer Corps"; in June, 1944, this
title was changed to "African Pioneer Corps," and in April,
1946, it was altered again to its present form—High Commission
Territories Corps.

A cross pattée (i.e. the Dannebrog) thereon in the centre a circle enclosing the letter "A", cypher of Queen Alexandra; above and resting upon the top arm of the cross, a crown; on either side of the cross a branch of laurel. On the lower portion of the left branch is inscribed "Sub Cruce" and on the lower portion of the right branch is inscribed "Candida". Below the cross and on the bottom of the branches a scroll inscribed "Q.A.R.A.N.C." For officers the badge is in gilt, except that the scroll is in silver plate, and for other ranks the corresponding metals are gilding metal and white metal.

THE DANISH CROSS (The Dannebrog—"The Strength of Denmark") has an interesting origin. King Waldemar fought a great battle with the Estonians in 1219, at the outset of which his army was on the point of being heavily defeated. The moment was critical, so Waldemar prayed to God for help. Immediately he saw a great White Cross in the sky on a blood-red ground. This he interpreted as a providential sign for him to renew the battle with the assurance of victory. He told his army of his vision, and with fortified strength they went forward to complete victory. Ever since then the White Cross on a red ground has been the blazon of the national flag of Denmark.

The Q.A.R.A.N.C. being successors to the Q.A.I.M.N.S., the central feature of the badge of the latter has been incorporated into the badge of the former.

The Corps button is a plain surface bearing in centre the cypher "A" of Her Majesty Queen Alexandra, surmounted by a crown: in gilt for officers and gilding metal for other ranks.

Laurel is associated with military glory, and therefore appropriate to the Corps.

On 1st February, 1949, the nursing service of the Army was placed upon a firm basis by being made a Corps of the Regular Army with the title "Queen Alexandra's Royal Army Nursing Corps," a tribute to the excellent work rendered by the Service for nearly a hundred years.

The formation of the Q.A.R.A.N.C. did not have the effect of automatically disbanding the Q.A.I.N.M.S., but this latter will gradually disappear, together with the Territorial Army Nursing Service, there being a T.A. element in the Q.A.R.A.N.C.

The Corps motto "Sub Cruce Candida" (Under the White Cross) refers to the Dannebrog (a white cross in a red field). In the badge, however, the cross is not white but gilt, which seems not in keeping with the motto.

CAP BADGE

COLLAR BADGE
(OFFICERS ONLY)

Cap badge: Within a laurel wreath surmounted by a crown, a Lioness rampant. For officers the laurel wreath and crown are in gilt metal and the Lioness in silver; for other ranks the corresponding metals are gilding metal and white metal. Collar badge: A Union Rose, thereon "WRAC"; the whole surmounted by a crown. The collar badge is worn by officers only and is made in gilt metal. Button: A plain surface bearing in the centre the cypher "M" of H.R.H. The Princess Royal, Controller-Commandant of the W.R.A.C., enfiled with the Princess's Coronet.

HER MAJESTY THE QUEEN honoured the Auxiliary Territorial Service by becoming its Commandant-in-Chief in August, 1939.

In view of the excellent services rendered by the A.T.S. during the World War of 1939-1945, the authorities decided to form a

Regular Corps of a similar nature, and to this end the Women's Royal Army Corps was formed on 1st February, 1949, with Her Majesty the Queen as Commandant-in-Chief.

The Princess Royal had been Controller-Commandant of the A.T.S. from 19th July, 1941, and became Controller-Commandant of the W.R.A.C. from its formation. H.R.H.'s long and close association with both Service and Corps is emphasized in the design of the W.R.A.C. button.

The laurel wreath and crown in the cap badge of the W.R.A.C. are taken from that of the A.T.S. and indicate their continuity.

The Lioness is the female counterpart of the lion, which appears in regimental badges, and is therefore symbolic of the service of women. This is the only instance of a lioness appearing in an Army badge.

The Union Rose is a Royal badge, and is therefore appropriate to a Royal Corps.

NON-COMBATANT CORPS

The letters "NCC" in gilding metal.

THE NON-COMBATANT CORPS was formed in April, 1940.

THE ROYAL MILITARY ACADEMY
SANDHURST

*In September, 1947, the following design was approved:
The Royal Cypher "GR VI" within a circle inscribed
"Royal Military Academy Sandhurst"; below the circle a
scroll inscribed with the motto "Serve to Lead"; the whole
surmounted by a crown. In white metal.*

WHEN THE Royal Military Academy, Woolwich, was amalgamated with the Royal Military College, Sandhurst, under the title "The Royal Military Academy Sandhurst," a new design of badge for wear by the cadets became necessary.

All entrants to the R.M.A. must serve in the ranks a minimum of four months before beginning their Officer Cadet training. Successful candidates are enlisted on Regular Army engagements as soon as possible after the final results of the examination are announced and sent to Arms Basic Training Units.

Before 1940 future officers of the Royal Artillery, Royal Engineers and Royal Signals were trained at the Royal Military Academy, Woolwich, and future Cavalry and Infantry officers, and others, at the Royal Military College, Sandhurst.

ARMY APPRENTICES SCHOOL

A pierced cog-wheel upon which is superimposed a cross, crossed swords and a flaming torch, the whole surmounted by a crown; below, a scroll inscribed "Army Apprentices School".

THERE ARE three Army Apprentices Schools (Chepstow, Arborfield and Harrogate), and their purpose is to train for the Regular Army tradesmen mainly for repair and construction trades such as armourers, fitters, electricians, surveyors, etc. Entrance to the schools is by examination of boys between generally 15 and 16½ years of age, who are required to enlist for twelve years, eight with the Colours and four on the reserve. The schools are administered directly by the War Office, through Commandants, assisted by administrative and instructional staffs. Whilst under training the boys are prepared for examinations of the London City and Guilds and the School Certificate. Each school is planned to take 1,000 on the boarding school principle.

DUKE OF YORK'S ROYAL MILITARY SCHOOL

The Royal Cypher within a circle inscribed "Royal Military School", surmounted by a crown. The badge is in gilding metal.

THIS SCHOOL was founded in June, 1801, by Field-Marshal Frederick, Duke of York, Commander-in-Chief of the British Army. It was situated in Chelsea, London, being opened in 1803. On a number of occasions in the nineteenth century proposals were made for dispersing the scholars and using the School as a barracks, but Queen Victoria would not approve them. In 1909, however, the School was moved to Guston, Dover. Entry into the School is restricted to sons of officers who have served in the ranks and those of warrant officers, N.C.Os. and men, or of ex-officers with rank service and ex-soldiers.

QUEEN VICTORIA'S SCHOOL, DUNBLANE

A Lion sejant full-faced, crowned, holding in the dexter paw a sword and in the sinister a fleur-de-lis, seated upon the Imperial Crown, the whole within a wreath of thistles and acorns. On the lower part of the wreath a scroll inscribed "Queen Victoria School". The Lion sejant is from the Royal Arms as used in Scotland. The badge is in silver.

THE SCHOOL was founded in 1903 as a memorial to Her Majesty Queen Victoria and to the Scottish sailors and soldiers who fell in the war in South Africa, 1899-1902.

Admission is open to boys of nine years of age who are sons of soldiers who are serving or who have served in Scottish regiments and of Scotsmen who are serving or who have served in any Regular branch of the Naval, Military or Air Forces.

ROYAL HOSPITAL, CHELSEA

The Rose and Thistle conjoined on one stalk on a solid circle within the Garter surmounted by a crown; below the Garter a straight scroll inscribed "Royal Hospital", and below this another straight scroll inscribed "Chelsea". The badge is in gilding metal. It is worn by the staff of ex-Warrant Officers, N.C.Os. and men, but not by the pensioners.

IN 1719 a regiment was formed from the Out-Pensioners of the Royal Hospital, which was designated "The Invalids." In 1751 this regiment was described as the "41st Foot, The Invalids," and was granted as a badge on its Colours the Rose and Thistle. (At that time Ireland had not joined the Union, hence the absence of the Shamrock.) This regiment is now The Welch Regiment.

The above badge was introduced in 1945 for the Royal Hospital Staff, and the connection with The Invalids is maintained in the central device.

Within a wreath of oak leaves a circle inscribed "King's Own Malta Regiment" and ensigned with the Imperial Crown; within the circle a Maltese cross on a parti-coloured white and red background; on the bottom of the wreath a straight scroll inscribed "MDCCC".

THE CIRCLE bearing the regimental title is in blue enamel, and the inscription thereon is in gilt lettering; the Maltese cross is in silver, and the background is vertically divided equally white on the left side and red on the right side, white and red being the colours in the flag and Arms of Malta. The scroll on the bottom of the wreath is also in blue enamel and the letters "MDCCC" in gilt, this being the date A.D. 1800, which is explained by Army Order 441 of 1889, which reads as follows:

"Her Majesty The Queen has been graciously pleased to permit the Royal Malta Militia to bear the date '1800' as a distinction in commemoration of the services of the Malta Militia during the siege of Valetta." Under the authority of Army Order 295 of 1924, this unique honour is borne by The King's Own Malta Regiment.

"Long-established tradition has it that the red and white were the colours of the Norman House of Hauteville, and that the flag and the corresponding Arms are one of the legacies of Roger of Hauteville, Count of Sicily, Lord of Malta, to this smallest of his dominions" ("Malta," by Sir Harry Luke, K.C.M.G., etc., p. 24). Roger de Hauteville took Malta from the Arabs in 1090.

ROYAL WEST AFRICAN FRONTIER FORCE

A palm tree standing on a mount, below which is a scroll inscribed "R.W.A.F.F".

THE R.W.A.F.F. consists of The Nigeria Regiment, The Gold Coast Regiment, The Sierra Leone Battalion and The Gambia Company. There was a Lagos Battalion dating from 1862, which took part in the Ashanti War of 1873-4 as the Lagos Constabulary and earned for the R.W.A.F.F. its first battle honour: in 1906 it became the 2nd Bn. Southern Nigeria Regiment. In 1914 the Northern and Southern Nigeria Regiments were amalgamated under the present title of "The Nigeria Regiment." The Gold Coast Regiment is descended from the Gold Coast Constabulary and the Sierra Leone Battalion from the Sierra Leone Frontier Police. The Gambia Company was raised in 1901.

The Sierra Leone Battalion and the Gambia Company are now designated Sierra Leone Regiment and Gambia Regiment respectively. The raising of their status to that of a regiment does not involve the formation of a number of new battalions for the present.

THE KING'S AFRICAN RIFLES

A bugle with strings, a crown above the strings and a scroll below the bugle inscribed "The King's African Rifles".

BEFORE 1904 there were a number of local Corps in East Africa, such as the East African Rifles and Uganda Rifles, which dealt with local risings. As necessity arose these forces were reinforced from India—a slow and expensive method. In 1904 the Indian contingents were withdrawn and a purely African Force formed called "The King's African Rifles," the 1st and 2nd Battalions being the re-formed Nyasaland units and the 3rd and 4th Battalions the old East African Rifles and Uganda Rifles respectively. Although a Rifle Corps, the K.A.R. carries Colours, the first battle honour thereon being "Ashanti, 1900," indicating that its early service was not confined to East Africa. For the Great War, 1914-18, the regiment raised no fewer than twenty-two battalions.

During the late war of 1939-45 the regiment raised over fifty battalions which served in the operations in the Middle East and Burma.

A Camel in motion, seated thereon a soldier of the S.D.F. holding a rifle in his right hand and a rein in his left hand; behind his back is a portion of a spear; the whole upon a tablet inscribed "S.D.F". The badge is in white metal.

THE S.D.F. was formed in 1925. It played a striking part in repelling the Italian invasion of the Middle East in 1940. It served with distinction at Keren and Agordat, and also at Kufra and Jalo, before serving in the Eighth Army in the advance to Tripoli and Tunis. Its wartime strength approximated to 30,000.

The S.D.F. is commanded by the Kaid, at present a Major-General seconded from the British Army. A proportion of British officers and N.C.Os. also serve with it, but the Sudanization of the Force is in progress.

The Headquarters are at Khartoum, and the S.D.F. comprises four Corps—viz., Camel Corps, Eastern Arab Corps, Western Arab Corps and Equatorial Corps—together with the usual supporting arms, Engineers, Service Corps and Signals.

THE MALAY REGIMENT

Within a circle inscribed "Ta'at dan Stia" (Loyal and True) in Jawi characters, a kris and its sarong (scabbard) crossed; above the circle an Oriental crown; below the circle a scroll inscribed "Askar Melayu" (The Malay Regiment) also in Jawi characters; supporting the circle on each side, a tiger. The badge is in gilding metal for all ranks.

AN EXPERIMENTAL company was formed at Port Dickson, Federated Malay States, on 1st March, 1933, and from this small beginning it was expanded to the strength of a battalion by 1939. A second battalion was formed on 1st December, 1941, and both battalions fought with distinction against the Japanese in the Malayan Campaign.

The 1st Battalion was raised by Major G. McI. S. Bruce, M.C., and the 2nd by Major F. W. Young, both of The Royal Lincolnshire Regiment.

At present (1950) the regiment is organized in four battalions, a Depot and a Brigade Headquarters. The usual ancillary troops from R.A.S.C., R.A.O.C., etc., are attached to the regiment.

A shield charged with two Lions (or Leopards) passan guardant, one above the other, with crown above; below, a scroll inscribed "Cyprus Regiment". In bronze for officers and gilding metal for other ranks.

THE SHIELD charged with the two Lions is the Arms of Cyprus and is derived from a seal of Richard I, who took possession of the island and married Berengaria of Navarre there in 1191.

The regiment was formed in April, 1940, and was disbanded on 31st March, 1950 (A.O. 35/1950).

Early in the late war great numbers of Cypriots expressed a desire to serve the Mother Country in some active manner, and this expression of loyalty was given expression by the formation of The Cyprus Regiment in April, 1940. Many Cypriots were already serving in various regiments and corps, and those who wished were permitted to transfer to their own regiment, whose organization included Mechanical Transport and Pack Transport Companies, Infantry and Pioneer Companies.

THE PALESTINE REGIMENT

*A vertical olive tree within a circle inscribed "Palestine" in
English, Hebrew and Arabic. The officers' badges were in
bronze and other ranks' in gilding metal.*

THE PALESTINE REGIMENT was formed in September, 1942, and
disbanded in August, 1948.

The original members were Palestinians normally resident in
Palestine, and it was composed during its brief existence of
British, Jewish and Arabic nationals, a fact which is reflected in
the languages of the word "Palestine" in the badge. In Novem-
ber, 1944, a Jewish Brigade Group was organized from the
Jewish battalions of the regiment.

*Extract from despatch by General Sir H. Maitland Wilson on the
operations in the Middle East from 16th February, 1943, to
8th January, 1944 (Reprinted, by permission of H.M. Station-
ery Office, from "London Gazette," No. 37786 of Wednesday,
13th November, 1946):*

Para. 325.—During November, 1943, the authorized badge for
the Palestine Regiment became available for issue, and twenty
soldiers of the 1st (Jewish) Battalion, the Palestine Regiment,
and forty-nine from the 3rd Battalion refused to accept or to

wear the badge. All these men were tried by Court Martial for disobeying a lawful command. In every case the defence took the line that it was against the men's religious principles and their conscience to wear the badge. They were all found guilty and given sentences varying from forty-five to sixty days' field punishment. It was obvious that this wholesale refusal was prompted by political considerations, and on investigation it was ascertained that all the accused were members of the Revisionist Party. In an interview with the General Officer Commanding in Palestine the head of the political branch of the Jewish Agency expressed the view that the incident was a stupid demonstration by a minor group and that their attitude was not supported by the Jewish Agency.

APPENDICES

APPENDIX ONE

THE GARTER

THE GARTER in badges is a representation of the Garter in the insignia of the Most Noble Order of the Garter. This Order was established by King Edward III in 1348 and it is the premier Order of Great Britain.

The Garter is made of dark blue velvet, upon which is borne, in gold lettering, the motto of the Order, viz., Honi Soit Qui Mal y Pense.

A circle, or strap with buckle, inscribed with the regimental title or motto, other than the Garter motto, is not a garter. In badges the Garter may only correctly be described as such when it contains the motto of the Order of the Garter.

THE CASTLE AND KEY OF GIBRALTAR

DURING THE War of the Spanish Succession Gibraltar was captured in July, 1704, after a three-day siege, by forces under the command of Admiral Sir George Rooke. Eight British regiments have been granted the Battle Honour "Gibraltar, 1704-5" in commemoration of their service on this occasion.

The British remained in possession of The Rock, without such possession being seriously disputed as far as resort to arms was concerned, until 1779, when Spain, later joined by France, commenced a siege. At that time the Governor was General Sir George Augustus Eliott (later Lord Heathfield), a soldier of great character and distinction.

At that time Great Britain's main preoccupation was in America, where the War of Independence was being fought, and it occurred to her enemies that this would be a favourable time to oust her from Gibraltar.

Repeated efforts were made to dislodge the small British garrison, but all failed. Early in 1782 an officer in the Royal Artillery invented a new form of gun-carriage wheel, which allowed a large angle of depression of the gun to be given, and this proved invaluable to the defence of the Rock.

A combined Spanish and French attack took place in July, 1782, but Eliott, by using red-hot shot, burnt or sank all of the enemy's battering ships. This was the last serious attack on the fortress and the long siege came to an end in February, 1783.

Under Horse Guards letters of 1784 the honour "Gibraltar" was granted to:

> 12th Foot—now The Suffolk Regiment.
>
> 39th Foot—now The Dorsetshire Regiment (1st Battalion).
>
> 56th Foot—now The Essex Regiment (2nd Battalion).
>
> 58th Foot—now The Northamptonshire Regiment (2nd Battalion).

On various dates between 1827 and 1836 "The Castle and Key" and the motto "Montis Insignia Calpe," being part of the Armorial bearings of Gibraltar, were added to "Gibraltar, 1779-83." In the case of The Essex Regiment the date is "1779-82."

Under Army Order 73 of 1908 the honour was extended to The Highland Light Infantry, where the date is "1780-83."

The above-mentioned badges were granted for bearing on Regimental Colours; and with the exception of the date after "Gibraltar" they have been incorporated into the regimental clothing badges of the first four regiments.

The "Castle and Key" with the motto "Montis Insignia Calpe" (the Arms of Gibraltar) were granted by Henry IV of Castile in 1462 after the Duke of Medina had captured the place from the Moors. The key is an allusion to the fact that the rock is the "Key to the Mediterranean."

EGYPTIAN CAMPAIGN OF 1801

IN OCTOBER, 1800, the British Government decided that the French Force in Egypt should be expelled because it constituted a threat to our communications with India. Accordingly a force was assembled in the Mediterranean under the command of Sir Ralph Abercromby, whilst Lord Keith commanded the fleet to co-operate with it.

The French were originally commanded by General Kleber, but when he was assassinated in May, 1800, General Menou succeeded him.

The British force made a successful landing in Aboukir Bay, east of Alexandria, on 8th March, 1801, mainly due to the energy and gallantry of Major-General Sir John Moore, later of Corunna fame. Abercromby advanced his line on 13th March, and was opposed again by the French, whose right flank rested on the eastern end of Lake Mareotis. Being again successful, he pressed forward towards Alexandria, where the main French force lay, but eventually occupied the late French position, which he proceeded to strengthen.

The British force was organized as follows:

Guards Brigade (Major-General Ludlow)—1st Coldstream, 1st Scots.

1st Brigade (Major-General Coote)—2nd R. Scots, two battalions 54th.

2nd Brigade (Major-General Craddock)—8th, 13th, 18th, 90th.

3rd Brigade (Major-General Lord Cavan)—50th, 79th.

4th Brigade (Brigadier-General Doyle)—2nd, 30th, 44th, 89th.

5th Brigade (Brigadier-General John Stuart)—Minorca Regiment, De Roll's, Dillon's.

Reserve (Major-General Moore, Brigadier-General Oakes)—23rd, 28th, 42nd, 58th, four companies 40th, Corsican Rangers.

Cavalry Brigade (Brigadier-General Finch)—1 troop 11th L.D., 12th, 26th and Hompesch's L.D.

Artillery—about 700 of all ranks.
(*Vide* Fortescue, Vol. IV, Part II, p. 819.)

Following the action on 13th March, skirmishes between the opposing sides continued, and the French built up their forces with the intention of making a surprise attack on Abercromby. The British commander had an idea that Menou would probably attack him at night and he consequently issued orders to meet such a contingency.

Before daylight on 21st March the French attacked. At this time the British Force was disposed as follows, by Brigades: Craddock on extreme left, Coote, Guards, Stuart, Moore, with four gunboats protecting the right flank. Cavan was on the left behind Craddock and Doyle was behind Stuart, with the cavalry behind Coote. Three gunboats were on Lake Aboukir on the left.

The French made a feint attack on the left flank, but attacked in earnest the Roman Camp on the extreme right, occupied by the 28th and 58th, which were soon reinforced by other troops. In the darkness the enemy became very confused and during the tumult some of the French penetrated the British line and came up in rear of our position. The 28th and 42nd turned about and by their fire drove them into a building, where they were destroyed by the 23rd and 58th.

A French cavalry charge met a disastrous end, but the enemy infantry continued to attack grimly until overcome by the steady, accurate fire of the British which eventually routed them. Menou now sent his second line of cavalry to the charge in an endeavour to wrest the vital Roman Camp from Abercromby. Some of the squadrons broke through and came up on the rear of this redoubt, and Abercromby himself was for a short time made prisoner. The 28th faced about and disposed of the Dragoons in their rear and our other regiments decimated the remainder.

This was the beginning of the end, for the French, who eventually drew off about 9 a.m., were a thoroughly defeated army.

In July, 1801, a force, composed of the following regiments and corps, under the command of Major-General David Baird, arrived at Suez:

Royal Artillery
Bengal Horse Artillery
Bengal Foot Artillery

Madras Foot Artillery

Bombay Foot Artillery

Royal Engineers

Bengal Engineers ⎫

Madras Engineers ⎬ only a few officers from these Corps

Bombay Engineers ⎭

Madras Engineers

8th Light Dragoons (later Hussars)

6th Foot (Royal Warwickshire Regiment)

10th Foot (Royal Lincolnshire Regiment)

80th Foot (2nd South Staffordshire Regiment)

86th Foot (2nd Royal Ulster Rifles)

88th Foot (1st Connaught Rangers)

Bengal Volunteers, Native Infantry

1st Bombay Regiment

7th Bombay Regiment

In July, 1801, also, a troop (dismounted) of the 8th Light Dragoons with the 61st Foot (2nd Gloucestershire Regiment) arrived at Suez from the Cape and joined the Indian Contingent.

The whole of General Baird's command moved towards Alexandria, via Cairo, and took part in the concluding operations of the campaign.

Abercromby was wounded during the action on 21st March and died as a result on 28th March, 1801. He was succeeded by General Hutchinson, who brought the campaign to a victorious conclusion in the following August.

By Horse Guards Circular Letter No. 170, dated 6th July, 1802, the badge of the Sphinx superscribed "Egypt" was granted to the regiments that took part in the campaign, some of whom have since incorporated them into their regimental badges.

As to the type of Sphinx that would be appropriate to commemorate a campaign in Egypt, one would have thought that an Egyptian Sphinx would be used. In this case it is not so. The distinctive points of an Egyptian Sphinx are that it is exclusively male, has a beard and its tail lies *on* its back, as opposed to pointing up *over* its back. The Sphinx of Thothmes III at Cairo is a correct

Egyptian type: it had a beard originally but that has been worn away. The Sphinxes flanking Cleopatra's Needle on the Thames Embankment, London, are practically identical with that of Thothmes III, except that they have no beard. (These details were kindly furnished by the late Dr. H. R. Hall, Keeper of Egyptian Antiquities, British Museum.)

In view of the above, none of the Sphinxes borne on the Colours or in the badges of British regiments is correct, for none has a beard, a number are obviously female as shown by their breasts, and have the tail pointing up over the back.

THE WHITE HORSE OF HANOVER

TOWARDS THE end of his reign, King Charles II (1660-1685) became more openly a Roman Catholic and on his deathbed was received into that faith. He was succeeded by his brother, James II (1685-1688), a bigoted Roman Catholic. As Great Britain was predominantly Protestant, this sharp difference between Crown and people was the cause of much trouble. Eventually in 1688 the people drove out James and invited his son-in-law, the Protestant Prince William of Orange, who had married the Princess Mary, to occupy the throne, which he did and became William III.

To ensure that the Crown should not again pass to a Roman Catholic an Act of Settlement was drawn up and became law in 1701. Under this it was enacted that in default of issue to William III (1689-1702) or Queen Anne (1702-1714), the Crown was to pass to "The Most Excellent Princess Sophia, Electress and Duchess of Hannover," a granddaughter of James I, and to "the heirs of her body, being Protestants."

It was further enacted "That whoever shall hereafter come to the possession of this Crown shall join in communion with the Church of England as by law established."

By these enactments James II's son and heir, Prince James, being a Roman Catholic, was excluded from the succession. He became known as the Old Pretender.

In the spring of 1708 a French expedition sailed from Dunkirk, with Prince James on board, with a view to landing in Scotland to stir up the Jacobite cause. It reached the Firth of Forth, but failed to make a landing owing to the activities of the English fleet under Sir George Byng, and returned to Dunkirk.

On the death of Queen Anne on 1st August, 1714, George, the son of Sophia of Hanover, mentioned in the Act of Settlement, became heir to the throne, his mother having died in the previous June.

Towards the end of her reign Queen Anne was lending support to the Jacobite cause, a fact which the Pretender made known publicly immediately after her death, and his supporters in Scotland hastened their secret preparations for overthrowing the new king before he became firmly established on the throne. The Government, however, were fully aware of these moves, and the army was considerably increased to meet them. Of the regiments raised at that time only the following remain:

Wynne's Dragoons	...	9th Lancers
Gore's Dragoons	...	10th Hussars
Honeywood's Dragoons		11th Hussars
Bowles's Dragoons	...	12th Lancers
Munden's Dragoons	...	13th Hussars (now 13th/18th Hussars)
Dormer's Dragoons	...	14th Hussars (now 14th/20th Hussars)

On 6th September, 1714, the Earl of Mar raised the standard of revolt at Braemar on behalf of the Pretender and the opposing forces prepared for battle, but a year was to pass before active operations were undertaken. A portion of Mar's force remained under his command just north of Stirling whilst the remainder crossed the border and got as far as Preston in Lancashire, having met with little resistance on the way. On the same day, 13th November, 1715, battles took place both at Preston and Sheriffmuir, the latter a few miles north of Stirling. At Preston the rebels capitulated without much of a struggle, but the result of Sheriffmuir was doubtful, both sides claiming a victory. In any case the revolt collapsed and there was no more fighting.

Some regiments that have the White Horse of Hanover as a badge state that it was granted for service to King George in the 1715 Rebellion. In the absence of a definite authority to this effect there must be some doubt about the matter when it is remembered that, under the Royal Warrant for Clothing of 1st July, 1751, the grenadiers of all regiments of Infantry of the Line were ordered to wear "the White Horse" with motto over it, on the "little flaps" of the grenadier caps. Further, in the case of the Cavalry, under the Royal Warrant for Clothing of 19th December, 1768, the King's, or First, Standard or Guidon of each regiment was to bear "the White Horse" in a compartment in the first or fourth corner. It may be that the ancestor of the present "White Horse" borne by some regiments goes back no farther than the middle of the eighteenth century or a little later (1751-1768).

THE BUGLE

THE ORIGINAL role in the field of all Rifle and Light Infantry regiments (latter half of eighteenth and early part of the nine-teenth-century wars in North America and Peninsula mainly) was to skirmish or scout well ahead of the main body. For this duty all cumbersome equipment was dispensed with and the men equipped as "light" as possible. Normally, the drum was used for conveying orders in the field, but as this somewhat obstructed rapid movement it was discarded in favour of the bugle. Hence the bugle is now incorporated into the badges of Rifle and Light Infantry regiments as a link with their original role.